THE ECONOMICS OF MEDICAID

THE ECONOMICS OF MEDICAID

Assessing the Costs and Consequences

EDITED BY JASON J. FICHTNER

An earlier version of chapter 3 was published by Jason J. Fichtner and John Pulito as "Medicaid Overview" (Mercatus Research, Mercatus Center at George Mason University, Arlington, VA, December 11, 2013), available online at http://mercatus.org/publication/medicaid-overview.

Mercatus Center at George Mason University
3434 Washington Boulevard, 4th Floor
Arlington, VA 22201

Library of Congress Cataloging-in-Publication Data

The economics of Medicaid : assessing the costs and consequences / edited by Jason J. Fichtner.
p. ; cm.
Includes index.
ISBN 978-0-9892193-6-5 (paperback) -- ISBN 978-0-9892193-7-2 (kindle)
I. Fichtner, Jason J., editor of compilation. II. Mercatus Center, issuing body.
[DNLM: 1. United States. Patient Protection and Affordable Care Act. 2. Medicaid--economics. 3. Health Care Reform--economics--United States. 4. Health Policy--economics--United States. W 250 AA1]
RA412.4
368.4'200973--dc23
2014003886

Printed in USA

CONTENTS

"Medicaid pays the full freight for most healthcare services (with few out of pocket costs) but compensates by sanding down the rates paid to providers. The result is that the Medicaid benefit has been hollowed out over time. Fewer doctors are willing to see Medicaid patients, making it hard for patients to get appointments and schedule needed services."
—Scott Gottlieb, MD, practicing physician and
resident fellow at the American Enterprise Institute

"I want poor people in this country to have the kind of quality of care and dignity that members of Congress have."
—Senator Ron Wyden, D-Oregon

"Originally created to serve the poorest and sickest among us, the Medicaid program has grown dramatically but still doesn't include the kind of flexibility that states need to provide better health care for the poor and disadvantaged."
—Representative Fred Upton, R-Michigan

INTRODUCTION

JASON J. FICHTNER

Medicaid is now the largest health insurance provider in the United States. Unlike Medicare, which was created to provide health care coverage to those over the age of 65, Medicaid's intent was the provision of care for financially limited individuals of any age. As the chapters in this book will make clear, government health care spending is already at unprecedented levels, and its costs are expected to increase dramatically.

The Congressional Budget Office (CBO) estimates that by 2024, 20 million new people will be added to Medicaid (and the Children's Health Insurance Program) under the Patient Protection and Affordable Care Act (ACA)—an increase of nearly 30 percent. Further, according to the CBO, federal spending on Medicaid is already projected to rapidly increase under the ACA, from $265 billion in fiscal year (FY) 2013 to $574 billion in FY2024. Additionally, because Medicaid is actually run by each individual state with major funding assistance from federal cost-sharing dollars, state costs devoted to Medicaid are also expected to become much more burdensome. In terms of total state expenditures, Medicaid is the largest item in states' budgets—and will only get larger.

Given that the ACA is still in its infancy, and regulatory and legislative changes may occur in the near future to address problems with the initial rollout and implementation of the ACA, it is imperative to consider how significantly the ACA will further negatively impact federal and state budgets and affect the economy at large.

This book examines the economics of Medicaid and discusses the costs and consequences of a program that ends up providing poor-quality care at high costs. Part 1 deals with the challenges facing the Medicaid program. In chapter 1 Joe Antos describes the **structure of Medicaid**, including how the program is operated by each individual state yet is jointly financed by the federal governments and states. Antos examines the perverse incentives and negative effects this type of financing arrangement creates; namely, that states have adopted creative financing schemes to take advantage of loopholes to claim excess federal dollars. Further, Antos discusses how poorer states that actually need the most help in financing coverage for low-income populations are the least able to take advantage of the federal matching money by expanding their Medicaid programs. He also addresses what becomes a clear theme throughout the book, that there exists limited access to high-quality care and numerous disincentives to reducing the costs of Medicaid.

Former director of the CBO June O'Neill provides an account of **Medicaid's cost drivers** in chapter 2, noting that while Medicaid costs have grown with the increase in eligible participants, the composition of the Medicaid population has shifted. The number of children and working-age adults receiving benefits has rapidly increased to almost three-fourths of total beneficiaries, yet these groups incur relatively low per capita medical costs, and thus account for only one-third of total Medicaid expenditures. Meanwhile, the number of disabled beneficiaries, who also employ high-cost services, has grown rapidly.

Part 2 deals with Medicaid's budgetary impact. In chapter 3, I discuss **the federal side of the budget equation**, and Nina Owcharenko details **the state side of the budget equation** in chapter 4. Both chapters examine the growth in costs associated with the Medicaid program. It becomes clear after reading these two chapters that Medicaid is on a fiscally dangerous trajectory that will only continue to crowd out the ability of the federal government and the states to pay for other government services.

Part 3 of the book focuses more on the ACA and Medicaid. In chapter 5, **"Medicaid under the Affordable Care Act,"** Charles Blahous discusses how the ACA dramatically expanded the number of people eligible for Medicaid and the financial incentives offered to the states to expand coverage. Blahous then describes the financial dilemma faced by the states on whether to expand Medicaid under the ACA. He also tackles the tricky question of whether the ACA will reduce or increase federal Medicaid costs and the impact the expansion will have on the federal budget.

Chapter 6 provides an interesting essay on the implications of Medicaid on the practice of medicine. Darcy Nikol Bryan delivers **a physician's perspective** as an obstetrician-gynecologist in California. Bryan provides an overview of the philosophical underpinnings of the debate about how to best provide health care to low-income people and then examines the tensions created by Medicaid in the practice of medicine. She then discusses that the focus on providing health insurance has shifted the focus away from health outcomes.

The final three chapters of the book more fully detail the health outcome failures caused by Medicaid and suggest possible reforms. Whereas the earlier chapters in the book also discuss possible reforms, these three chapters provide more in-depth analysis. James Capretta addresses the more mainstream reforms in chapter 7, **"Reforming Medicaid."** Capretta discusses "waiver" requests that states can propose to the federal government that allow the Department of Health and Human Services to "waive" certain Medicaid requirements. These waivers raise a fundamental question of whether states are being treated equitably and whether the waiver process needs to be reformed. He also describes potential Medicaid reforms such as block grants and per capita caps, concluding that the fundamental federal–state relationship of Medicaid is in need of reform.

In chapter 8, **"How to Achieve Sustainable Medicaid Reform,"** Thomas Miller goes a step further. He starts off quickly by pointing out the financial trouble Medicaid was in before the ACA and how the ACA will only exacerbate a troubled program. Miller takes issue with critics of the ACA who advocate simple repeal of the ACA and he further suggests that in order to make Medicaid sustainable, more serious reforms need to be adopted than those that are commonly suggested. In a more comprehensive look at reform, Miller suggests that our approach to health policy should support broader economic policy initiatives, such as work and saving incentives, to better help protect low-income people.

In the concluding chapter, Robert Graboyes looks at **Medicaid and health**, picking up where Miller left off. Graboyes discusses the efficacy of Medicaid and whether it is even capable in its current form of providing high-quality health care efficiently and with low cost. While discussing the more common approaches to Medicaid reform, Graboyes goes further and suggests that the only way to achieve better health care outcomes is by embracing the private market—whether within Medicaid or through an appropriate replacement to Medicaid.

With or without Medicaid eligibility expansion, Medicaid is on a trajectory to require increasing resources at state and federal levels of government, creating difficult budgetary tradeoffs for both unless major and significant reforms to Medicaid are implemented. At the same time, it is important to recognize that expanded coverage does not necessarily translate into better care, and Medicaid's care does not necessarily translate into better health. A growing body of evidence shows that Medicaid badly fails the enrollees it is designed to help. Given these uncertainties, it is an appropriate time to assess how effectively Medicaid as an institution is capable of improving or maintaining its recipients' health, and how the program itself can be improved. This book will discuss these challenges and possible reforms.

PART 1:
CHALLENGES FACING MEDICAID

CHAPTER 1: THE STRUCTURE OF MEDICAID

JOSEPH ANTOS

Medicaid is the primary means of financing health care for America's poor. The program is operated by each state and jointly financed by the federal and state governments under a matching arrangement. The federal government pays a portion of every bill submitted to it by the states, with no overall budget limit. On average, one dollar spent on Medicaid-covered health services costs the state 43 cents with the remainder paid by the federal government.[1] Those federal payments are accompanied by a complex set of regulations and requirements that limit the flexibility of states to run their own programs.

States are pulled in opposite directions as a result of this payment arrangement. On the one hand, states have an incentive to expand the generosity of their programs because the net cost to the state is significantly less than the full cost of the additional services provided to their low-income residents. On the other hand, states have balanced budget requirements that limit the amount they can finance from their own budgets for any Medicaid expansion.

States have responded to these financial incentives in predictable ways. Reflecting their greater budget capacity, wealthier states have expanded eligibility for Medicaid well beyond federal minimums. Poorer states that need more help covering the health costs of their low-income populations have been less able to take advantage of the federal matching money by expanding their Medicaid programs.

As will be explained later in this chapter, states have adopted creative financing schemes that take advantage of statutory and regulatory loopholes to claim excessive federal matching payments. An Urban Institute study shows that the effective federal match rate for some states may have increased from about 57 percent of Medicaid cost to as much as 86 percent through the use of such schemes.[2] This drives up federal spending for Medicaid, which is an open-ended entitlement that automatically pays its share of the bills submitted by the states—even when the states have not paid their full share.

Regardless of budget capacity, state Medicaid programs pay far less than Medicare or private insurers for health services. According to federal actuaries, Medicaid payment rates for inpatient hospital services in 2009 were about 66 percent of private health insurance payment rates.[3] Medicaid payment rates for physician services in 2008 averaged about 58 percent of private rates. These consistently low payments have limited Medicaid beneficiaries' access to medical services they have been promised.

Low payment rates do not translate into low spending by either the federal or state governments. The Congressional Budget Office (CBO) estimates that federal 2013 spending for Medicaid will total $265 billion.[4] Total spending, including by states, comes to $465 billion. Between 2000 and 2012, Medicaid spending grew 7 percent a year.[5] In contrast, the American economy grew only 4.2 percent annually over that period.[6]

Although this rapid growth in spending places an increasing burden on state budgets, regulatory barriers limit what states can do to reduce Medicaid costs and improve the delivery of health services to beneficiaries. Even relatively modest changes in program operations must be approved by the Centers for Medicare and Medicaid Services (CMS) in a process that can be time-consuming and uncertain. Moreover, because the federal government shares in the cost of Medicaid with the states, it also shares in any savings that the states achieve through better policies and more effective management. At least 50 cents of every dollar that is saved by the state must be turned over to the federal government. This discourages states from investing in changes that could make Medicaid a more efficient program.

The Patient Protection and Affordable Care Act (ACA) proposed to expand the number of people covered by Medicaid, but the legislation failed to change the financial incentives that produce second-class health care at first-class cost.[7] Structural reforms, including shifting from a matching grant to a modified block grant and allowing beneficiaries more freedom in how they use their Medicaid subsidy, are necessary to reduce unnecessary spending and promote high-quality, patient-centered care.

THE BASICS OF MEDICAID FINANCING

Medicaid pays for a broad range of health and long-term care services for low-income individuals, including children, persons with disabilities, and the elderly.[8] Some 72 million people will have received Medicaid benefits at some point during the year 2013.[9] Over the next decade, Medicaid will spend $7.5 trillion, with federal payments accounting for $4.3 trillion. Although it is a national program, states have some latitude to tailor Medicaid to meet local needs and preferences, including states' ability to finance public programs.

When Medicaid was enacted in 1965, states were given the option to participate. However, any state choosing not to participate would lose substantial federal subsidies to help cover the health care costs of low-income individuals who would otherwise be unable to pay their medical bills. Legally, Medicaid is voluntary. Practically, no state would consider dropping the program unless the federal government drastically cut its financial support.

Medicaid is a means-tested program; benefits are available only to people whose income and assets fall below certain levels. Not every low-income individual, however, is eligible for Medicaid. The federal government has established eligibility categories, such as being a low-income child, a pregnant woman, or an adult with dependent children. States must cover people in those groups, and many states have expanded Medicaid beyond minimum eligibility requirements established by the federal government. However, eligibility is not uniform, and certain groups (notably childless adults) have traditionally not been eligible for Medicaid.[10]

The ACA included a requirement that states expand coverage to at least all people with incomes up to 133 percent of the federal poverty level.[11] A state failing to comply would lose all federal funds for its Medicaid program. That provision was struck down as unconstitutionally coercive in a Supreme Court ruling, leaving any expansion of income eligibility standards up to the states.[12]

States are required to cover acute health services, including hospital and physician services; laboratory and imaging services; nursing facility and home health care; and family planning services. Most states offer optional services, including prescription drugs, dental care, durable medical equipment, and personal care services.

Medicaid is also an entitlement program. Individuals who are eligible for Medicaid have a legal right to payment for services offered under the program. States also have a legal right to federal matching payments for the services provided to eligible individuals. Congress can change federal payment obligations to state Medicaid programs only by changing program rules, including eligibility requirements and covered services. This budget treatment leaves Medicaid on automatic pilot, less likely to be in the legislative mix when federal deficits must be reduced.

The federal government shares in the cost that states incur for their Medicaid benefits. The federal medical assistance percentage (FMAP) for medical services, which determines the federal payment, is tied to state per capita income according to the following formula:

$$\text{FMAP} = 100\% - \left[\frac{(\text{State per capita income})^2}{(\text{US per capita income})^2} \times 0.45\right]$$

The law also provides that no state can have a match rate lower than 50 percent or higher than 83 percent of the cost of benefits.[13] If the match rate is 50 percent, the federal government and the state share equally in the cost of Medicaid services. If the match rate is 60 percent, the state pays 40 percent of the cost and the federal government pays the rest.

Because the FMAP is a percentage payment rather than a fixed dollar amount, it is a countercyclical program that automatically accounts for economic downturns or other state-specific circumstances (such as increasing cost or use of services) that drive up Medicaid spending. Federal payments keep pace with higher program costs without the need for legislation to adjust the formula. The FMAP is also designed to enable states with different fiscal capacities to provide roughly equivalent benefits, although that does not always work out in practice.

In 2013, Mississippi received the highest regular match, equal to 73.4 percent, while 14 high-income states (including New York and California) received a 50 percent match. The calculation is complicated by adjustments for states that experienced a major disaster (such as the 2010 oil spill in Louisiana) and increases to the matching percentage required under the ACA for states expanding Medicaid eligibility.

The 50 percent minimum match rate provides more funding to high-income states than they would otherwise receive according to the FMAP formula. The FMAP for those states would fall as low as 23 percent if not for the 50 percent floor.[14] However, it is doubtful that Medicaid could have been enacted into law without the FMAP floor, which ensured high-income states a politically acceptable return on the high taxes they pay to maintain the program.

Higher-income states have more generous Medicaid programs than low-income states, partly as a consequence of their richer economic base that enables them to draw down a greater share of federal dollars. Eight states—California, New York, Texas, Pennsylvania, Florida, Ohio, Michigan, and Illinois—received one-half of total federal Medicaid

Table 1. Eight Highest Recipients of Federal Medicaid Spending, 2011

State	Federal spending (millions)	Percentage of national spending	FMAP (%)
California	$33,935	12.58	50.00
New York	$30,198	11.19	50.00
Texas	$19,264	7.14	60.56
Pennsylvania	$13,228	4.90	55.64
Florida	$11,721	4.34	55.45
Ohio	$11,058	4.10	63.69
Michigan	$8,901	3.30	65.79
Illinois	$7,751	2.87	50.20
Total	$136,056	50.43	–
National	$269,800	100.00	63.40

Sources: Medicaid and CHIP Payment Access Commission, Report to the Congress on Medicaid and CHIP, *Washington, DC, March 15, 2012, 98–99, http://www.macpac.gov/reports; and Henry J. Kaiser Family Foundation,* Federal Medical Assistance Percentage (FMAP) for Medicaid and Multiplier, *Menlo Park, CA, http://kff.org/medicaid/state-indicator/federal-matching-rate-and-multiplier/#.*

funding in 2011 (table 1).[15] As a result, states in the Northeast and the West Coast tend to offer Medicaid to people higher up on the economic scale than states in the South.

Ten states have consistently received the 50 percent minimum match rate: California, Colorado, Connecticut, Maryland, Massachusetts, Minnesota, New Hampshire, New Jersey, New York, and Virginia (figure 1).[16] Nine of them cover children in families with incomes at least 250 percent of the federal poverty level (FPL), and eight cover working parents with incomes at least equal to the FPL.[17]

Ten states that have consistently received the highest FMAPs over the past decade (with average rates ranging from 77.6 to 71.0 percent) are Mississippi, West Virginia, Arkansas, New Mexico, Utah, Kentucky, Idaho, South Carolina, Alabama, and Montana.[18] Only three cover children in families with incomes at least 250 percent of the FPL, and none cover working parents with incomes at or above poverty.

Figure 1. Top 10 and Bottom 10 FMAP Averages, 2004–13

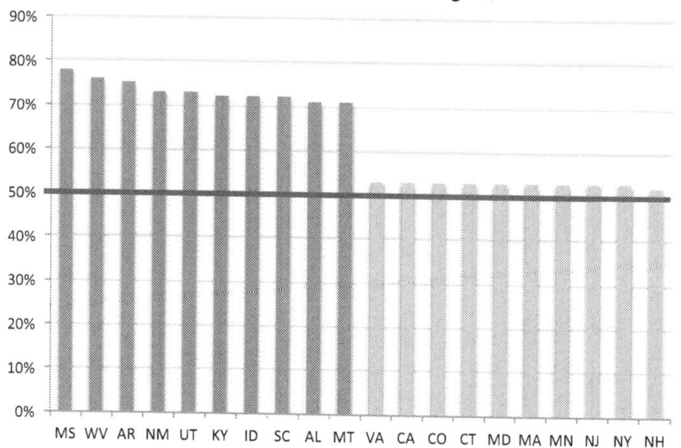

Source: Kaiser Family Foundation, Federal Medical Assistance Percentage (FMAP) for Medicaid and Multiplier, *http://kff.org/medicaid/state-indicator/federal-matching-rate-and-multiplier/.*

Financial incentives and each state's capacity to finance its share of Medicaid costs contribute to the variations in program generosity. But differences in political and philosophical views regarding the role of government also help explain variations across states. (For more on the budgetary impacts of Medicaid at the federal and state levels, see chapters 3 and 4, pages 49 and 65.)

DISINCENTIVES FOR REDUCING PROGRAM COST

The major recession in 2007 and 2008 and the slow recovery since have sharply increased the federal budget deficit. Revenues declined as the economy slumped, and stimulus spending drove up outlays. In September 2006, outstanding debt of the US government totaled \$8.5 trillion.[19] By September 2012, the debt had almost doubled, to \$16.1 trillion.

States, like the federal government, face increasing demands on their budgets. Unlike the federal government, states operate under a balanced budget rule and have limited ability to borrow their way out of fiscal distress.

Medicaid accounts for a major portion of state budgets. In fiscal year (FY) 2012, Medicaid represented 23.9 percent of state spending on average.[20] With the rising cost of health care and tighter budgets, the program has increased fiscal pressure on states. Perhaps surprisingly, Medicaid has not become a target for those looking to cut state budgets.

Because of the matching formula, states are reluctant to adopt cost-reducing policies in Medicaid. There is a built-in bias in favor of maintaining or expanding the program. If a state such as New York, with its 50 percent match rate, wished to cut its own Medicaid spending by $1 million, it would have to adopt policies that cut total Medicaid spending in the state by $2 million. Under the matching formula, half of the savings would accrue to the federal government.

The bias is even stronger for low-income states such as Mississippi, which had a 73.4 percent match rate in 2013. For the state to save $1 million, it would have to cut total spending by $3.8 million.

The financial terms facing a state seeking to cut its Medicaid spending are unfavorable. In most cases, a state reducing its spending will cut other programs that are paid by funds covered entirely by the state rather than Medicaid.

The political and technical challenges of reducing Medicaid spending are just as daunting. Reducing eligibility means informing certain individuals that they no longer have medical coverage. Reducing benefits means informing certain individuals that they must pay out of pocket for a service previously covered by Medicaid. Reducing payment rates to doctors and hospitals means further cuts in payments that already qualify as the lowest in the market.[21] Such cuts hit the financial bottom lines of providers who already feel underpaid, and threaten the already limited access to care for those in need.

Consequently, we rarely have seen widespread state action to reduce Medicaid spending despite the program's prominence in state budgets. A notable exception came in the wake of a temporary increase in federal subsidies for Medicare, which was part of the economic stimulus under the American Recovery and Reinvestment Act of 2009 (ARRA).[22] All states received a minimum 6.2 percentage point increase in their FMAPs starting in 2009. The increase was phased out during the first six months of 2011.

Although states recognized that the enhanced match rate was not likely to be extended indefinitely, they also had a strong incentive to take full advantage of the higher match while it was available. The recession led to increases in Medicaid spending and enrollment. Many states used the additional money to expand eligibility for the program and to delay implementing previously planned cost-cutting policies.[23]

The shift back to much lower match rates required most states to adopt aggressive cost-reducing policies.[24] Illinois limited Medicaid enrollees to no more than four prescriptions a month, imposed a copayment for prescriptions for adults who are not pregnant, eliminated nonemergency dental care for adults, and cut 25,000 adults from the rolls.[25] Other states cut pay for health care providers, eliminated coverage for optional services, imposed new fees for the routine use of hospital emergency rooms, and increased other payments made by Medicaid enrollees.

According to the National Governors Association and the National Association of State Budget Officers, 33 states either froze or cut provider payments in 2012.[26] Nineteen states limited benefits, and seven imposed additional copayments on enrollees.

Cutting program costs by finding more efficient ways to provide care to Medicaid patients is more desirable than cutting already-low provider payments or reducing benefits, but it is also difficult to accomplish and unlikely to yield budget savings in the short term. Eighteen states expanded managed care in 2012, and 14 states adopted other reforms of the delivery system. In addition, 31 states adopted stronger program integrity measures intended to reduce fraud and abuse in Medicaid billing.[27] Cost savings are possible by shifting Medicaid beneficiaries from a fee-for-service system to managed care. In a managed care delivery system, enrollees get most or all of their Medicaid services from an organization under contract with the state. Almost 50 million people receive benefits through some form of managed care, on either a voluntary or mandatory basis.[28]

The sharp drop in federal matching payments was an unprecedented event that forced states to take unprecedented action. The typical experience is less dramatic, with states making smaller adjustments to eke out moderate budget savings.

MAXIMIZING FEDERAL PAYMENTS

Do states actually pay their share of Medicaid expenses? On the face of it, the answer is yes. But the way states cover their costs has long been a source of controversy with the federal government.

States have used legal financing mechanisms to shift substantial costs to the federal government, local governments, and health care providers. By adopting various financing mechanisms, states can increase their effective match rates and reduce the amount they must pay out of their own budget. By reducing their reliance on general funds, states can circumvent balanced budget requirements, which otherwise limit the ability to expand their Medicaid programs.

States are required to adhere to broad federal guidelines regarding how they pay their share of Medicaid costs. Not surprisingly, states have a strong incentive to identify payment sources that maximize the federal payment. The rules are subject to interpretation, and states vary in their use of payment maximization techniques.

States can rely on several sources of funding for Medicaid, including general funds (revenue derived from personal and corporate income taxes and sales taxes), local government funds, provider taxes, and other sources.[29] Public attention has focused on several financing mechanisms that have been used—and in some cases, abused—to increase federal Medicaid payments to a state.[30]

States are permitted to tax providers to generate funds to cover part of the state's share of Medicaid costs.[31] Until the early 1990s, some states exploited this loophole in the law by using taxes on hospitals and nursing homes to generate federal matching payments. For example, hospitals might agree to pay $10 million in provider taxes in exchange for the state increasing Medicaid hospital reimbursement by $20 million. On balance, hospitals gain $10 million in revenue. If the FMAP is 60 percent, the federal government would pay an extra $12 million. That gives the state budget an extra $2 million that it would otherwise not have received.

Legislation limited, but did not eliminate, states' ability to draw down federal matching funds with provider tax revenue.[32] The provider tax must be broad-based and uniform to reduce the possibility of collusion. The tax revenue cannot exceed 25 percent of the state's share of program cost, and states cannot promise to reimburse providers.

Despite these restrictions, all 50 states used provider taxes to help finance Medicaid in 2013.[33] Following the previous example, a state can still impose $10 million in provider taxes but can increase Medicaid reimbursements by only $8 million.[34] With a 60 percent FMAP, the federal government pays $4.8 million that it would not have paid otherwise—less than the $12 million extra federal payment that was available in earlier times, but still worth the effort. The providers lose $2 million, but the state gains $6.8 million. The state can use that extra money for any purpose, including programs unrelated to Medicaid or health care.[35]

Other financing mechanisms create similar opportunities to increase the federal matching payment. States have used intergovernmental transfers (IGTs), disproportionate share hospital (DSH) payments, and upper payment limits (UPLs) to increase the federal share of Medicaid costs above the amount prescribed by the FMAP formula.[36]

A state may use IGTs, which are funds transferred from counties or other local government entities, to finance up to 60 percent of its Medicaid share. States can increase payments to nursing homes and other providers operated by a local government above their actual cost of operation, which allows the state to draw down a larger federal matching payment. The IGT mechanism can be used to transfer some or all of the extra Medicaid payment from the local government back to the state budget, leaving the local provider no worse off. As in the previous example, this method increases the effective match rate and provides the state with additional funding that can be used for any purpose.[37]

States provide supplementary payments to hospitals that serve large numbers of low-income and uninsured patients. States make DSH payments to county-owned hospitals, which increases their Medicaid spending and triggers a federal match.[38] Subsequently, states can use IGTs to recover a portion of the DSH payment. The net effect is to increase federal payments while providing some, but not all, of those funds to hospitals serving low-income populations.[39]

The federal government attempted to limit how much states can increase provider payment rates and thus curb some financing abuses. States have broad authority to set payment rates for Medicaid providers, but the total amount they can pay each category of provider is restricted by the UPL.[40] The UPL is a statewide budget cap on Medicaid provider payments, limiting them to no more than the estimated amount Medicare would have paid for the same services. The provider categories include several classes of hospitals, nursing homes, intermediate care facilities, and outpatient facilities.

Because Medicaid generally pays lower rates than Medicare, states have flexibility under the UPL to give substantial supplemental payments to particular hospitals or other providers without exceeding the aggregate budget cap for a provider category. In a 2012 study, the Government Accountability Office (GAO) found that 39 states made supplemental payments to 505 DSH hospitals.[41] Total Medicaid payments to those hospitals exceeded the cost of providing care to Medicaid patients by $2.7 billion. GAO raised concerns about whether these large additional payments were being used for Medicaid purposes.

The evidence is compelling that the federal government is paying more than its formula-based share of Medicaid costs. States have strong incentives to maximize federal payments, and complex federal rules provide ample opportunity for states to use creative financing solutions. A recent study suggests that those financing methods increase federal Medicaid spending by 5 percent—$12.5 billion in 2013 alone.[42]

The federal government has generally been one step behind the most aggressive states, closing loopholes in the rules or imposing limitations after a particular financing technique has been in widespread use. This is unavoidable under Medicaid's shared financing structure. Sensibly, states organize their programs to their own advantage, leaving the federal government to retrofit the regulations to close off unanticipated ways states have devised to increase federal payments.

LIMITED ACCESS TO CARE

Even the most ardent supporters of Medicaid recognize that the program is plagued by problems regarding access to care. Sara Rosenbaum of George Washington University points out that poor Americans have faced "a substantial vacuum in actual access to health care" despite Medicaid's coverage guarantee.[43] A major cause of that access problem is the low rates of participation in Medicaid among health care providers, which is the direct result of low payment rates and overly burdensome administrative practices that delay payment and add to the headaches of dealing with state bureaucracy.

Medicaid payments for medical services are much lower than those offered by other payers. Physicians receive about 58 percent of what private insurers pay for comparable services.[44] Even the uninsured are likely to pay more than Medicaid. In a study conducted by MIT economists Jonathan Gruber and David Rodriguez, nearly 60 percent of the 3,860 physicians surveyed reported higher fees from the uninsured than from Medicaid.[45] Low fees coupled with excessive paperwork and late payments make it difficult for physicians to accept Medicaid patients.[46]

Consequently, Medicaid patients have difficulty getting appointments with physicians. This results in delayed treatment, increasing the use of hospital emergency departments and increasing costs to the health system.

The 2008 Health Tracking Physician Survey found that only about half of all physicians will accept new Medicaid patients.[47] Internists were 8.5 times more likely to refuse to see a new Medicaid patient as they were to refuse a patient with private coverage. The 2011 National Ambulatory Medical Care Survey shows that 30 percent of physicians would refuse new Medicaid patients, but 92 percent would take new patients who pay their own bills without the administrative hassle of any insurance.[48] Another study confirms that the type of health insurance you have can determine the kind of care you receive. Researchers at the University of Pennsylvania called 273 specialty clinics to determine whether they would accept a child with coverage from Medicaid or Children's Health Insurance Program (CHIP).[49] In more than half of the calls, the child's insurance status was requested before the caller was told whether an appointment could be scheduled. No appointment was given to two-thirds of the children described as Medicaid or CHIP patients. Only 11 percent of children described as having Blue Cross Blue Shield coverage were refused an appointment.

With limited access to physician services, Medicaid patients are likely to put off seeking medical attention, and they are more likely to seek care through the hospital emergency department. The 2003 Community Tracking Survey shows that Medicaid beneficiaries use emergency rooms two to three times more than people with private insurance.[50] The ER is often the only place a Medicaid patient can receive care.

Poorer access to care leads to poorer health outcomes for Medicaid patients. This was clearly demonstrated by a groundbreaking study of 893,658 patients undergoing major surgical operations between 2003 and 2007.[51] The study, conducted by medical researchers from the University of Virginia Health System, found that Medicaid patients experienced worse outcomes than patients with private insurance, Medicare, or no coverage at all. Three measures of care quality were examined: the rate of in-hospital mortality, average length of hospital stay, and total cost.

Eight major surgical operations were studied, with the most frequent being coronary artery bypass graft, colectomy (bowel surgery), and hip replacement. The analysis controlled for age, gender, income, geographic region, type of surgical operation, and 30 comorbid conditions. These adjustments corrected for differences in patient populations that could explain variations in patient outcomes other than the quality of care provided by the surgical team. For example,

Table 2. Outcomes for Surgical Patients, Adjusted for Patient and Hospital Characteristics

Outcome	Private	Medicare	Uninsured	Medicaid
In-hospital mortality (vs. private insurance)	–	+54%	+74%	+97%
Length of stay (days)	7.38	8.77	7.01	10.49
Total cost per case	$63,057	$69,408	$65,667	$79,140
Memorandum: Number of observations	337,535	491,829	24,035	40,259

Source: Damien J. LuPar et al., "Primary Payer Status Affects Mortality for Major Surgical Operations," Annals of Surgery *252, no. 3 (2010): 544–51, Riverwoods, Il, http://www.ncbi.nlm.nih.gov/pmc/articles/PMC3071622/pdf/nihms279555.pdf.*

Medicare patients are older than other patient groups and more likely to be in poor health, which could lead to poorer outcomes.

Medicaid patients were almost twice as likely to die in the hospital following major surgery than those with private insurance and considerably more likely to die than Medicare patients or the uninsured (table 2). About 1.3 percent of the 337,000 privately insured patients in the sample died in the hospital following surgery. Medicaid patients were 97 percent more likely than privately insured patients to die. Medicare patients and the uninsured had better outcomes: they were, respectively, 54 percent and 74 percent more likely to die than those with private insurance.

Adjusting for differences among hospitals and patients (other than their insurance status), the average Medicaid patient stayed about three days longer in the hospital than those with private insurance. Longer lengths of stay for observationally equivalent patients are consistent with poorer patient outcomes.

Despite lower payment rates, the increased use of services made Medicaid costs higher than for patients with other coverage. Average Medicaid costs were just over $79,000 per surgery—25 percent higher than the cost incurred by privately insured patients, and substantially higher than the costs paid by Medicare patients or the uninsured.

These negative results are confirmed by other studies, which also show a greater frequency of late diagnosis (which reduces the chances for successful treatment) and higher mortality rates when comparing Medicaid patients to those with other coverage.[52] This is not surprising given the conflicting incentives facing states. States have kept provider payment rates substantially below market levels to reduce their own spending, but states have also used administrative measures to magnify the amount the federal government pays through the matching formula. An overhaul of Medicaid financing and governance is needed to improve the care delivered to beneficiaries, promote greater efficiency, and bring an honest accounting system to the program.

REFORMING MEDICAID

Medicaid is a federal–state partnership, but an uneasy one. States run their own programs, but they must satisfy a vast array of federal requirements that have been justified as protecting the interests of the poor, health care providers, and taxpayers. In fact, none of those interests are well-served.

Financing is the major reason the program does not perform well. Because of the matching payment mechanism, states must share the savings they could receive by adopting delivery system reforms (such as shifting from fee-for-service payment to managed care plans) that may not be popular with local health care providers. Even if that political resistance can be overcome, states must negotiate a waiver of federal Medicaid rules from CMS. That can be a lengthy, and ultimately fruitless, process.[53]

Matching payments partially insulate states from the rising cost of health care and reduce their willingness to make delivery system reforms. Replacing the matching grant formula with a fixed payment, and giving states freer rein to adopt reforms without having to seek permission from CMS for even small changes, would give states stronger financial incentives and greater ability to manage their programs responsibly.

Several state governors have indicated that they need more flexibility in running their programs before they would be willing to expand Medicaid coverage under the ACA—even with 100 percent funding for new enrollees for the first few years.[54] Governors from Nebraska, Tennessee, Virginia, and Wyoming claimed they would move Medicaid to a block grant and replace thousands of pages of regulatory micromanagement with clear objectives agreed to by both the federal government and the states. The head of the Texas Human Services Commission pointed out that allowing states to manage for results would make better use of Medicaid dollars and support local solutions to local problems.[55]

A block grant creates a fixed grant from the federal government to the states, which is indexed for general inflation and population growth.[56] (For a more detailed explanation of the mechanics of block grants, see chapter 7, page 138.) Unlike the federal matching payment, a block grant would not increase as program spending increases (through either increased enrollment or rising costs of medical services).

An alternative to a block grant is a per capita cap. This approach would fix the federal subsidy amount for each enrollee rather than the payment made to the state for all Medicaid enrollees. Akin to a capitation payment made to health maintenance organizations, a per capita federal payment gives states strong incentives to control unnecessary costs without penalizing them if enrollment increases (and without making excess federal payments if enrollment drops).

Per capita cap proposals have recently been advanced as a solution to the perverse financial incentives of the current system.[57] Such proposals can be designed to account for differences in populations covered by Medicaid and other factors outside the direct control of the state that could increase program costs. Some enrollee groups, including those who need long-term care services and supports, have significantly higher Medicaid costs than average enrollees. Setting separate payment rates for such groups can more accurately track the program costs and ensure equitable cost-sharing between states and the federal government.

CONCLUSION

Medicaid is the largest public health program for low-income Americans. The ACA relies on a greatly expanded Medicaid program to provide health coverage for an additional 12 million people over the next two years—a 30 percent increase in national enrollment.[58] That expansion will increase federal spending by $710 billion through 2023, adding greatly to a worsening fiscal situation for both the federal and state governments.

Those additional enrollees will be joining a program in need of reform. Spending is high, but low provider payment rates reduce patient access to providers and necessary care. Federal financing arrangements must be reformed if we hope to slow the growth of Medicaid spending and improve program performance.

NOTES

1. Kaiser Commission on Medicaid and the Uninsured, *The Medicaid Program at a Glance*, March 2013, http://kff.org/medicaid/fact-sheet/the-medicaid-program-at-a-glance-update/.

2. Teresa A. Coughlin, Stephen Zuckerman, and Joshua McFeeters, "Restoring Fiscal Integrity to Medicaid Financing?," *Health Affairs* 26, no. 5 (2007): 1469–1480, http://content.healthaffairs.org/content/26/5/1469.full.

3. John D. Shatto and M. Kent Clemens, "Projected Medicare Expenditures under Illustrative Scenarios with Alternative Payment Updates to Medicare Providers" (Baltimore, MD: CMS Office of the Actuary, May 18, 2012), http://www.cms.gov/Research-Statistics-Data-and-Systems/Statistics-Trends-and-Reports/Reports TrustFunds/Downloads/2012TRAlternativeScenario.pdf.

4. Congressional Budget Office, *Medicaid—May 2013 Baseline*, May 14, 2013, http://www.cbo.gov/publication/44204.

5. Author's calculation based on Congressional Budget Office, *Historical Budget Data*, February 5, 2013, http://www.cbo.gov/publication/43904.

6. Author's calculation based on Bureau of Economic Analysis, *National Income and Product Accounts Tables*, Washington, DC, revised July 21, 2013, http://www.bea.gov/national/index.htm.

7. Patient Protection and Affordable Care Act, Pub. L. No. 111-148, 124 Stat. 119 (2010) (codified as amended sections of 42 U.S.C.); Office of the Legislative Counsel, *Compilation of Patient Protection and Affordable Care Act as Amended through May 1, 2010*, May 2010, http://www.google.com/url?sa=t&rct=j&q=&esrc=s&source=web&cd=2&ved=0CDMQFjAB&url=http%3A%2F%2Fhousedocs.house.gov%2Fenergycommerce%2Fppacacon.pdf&ei=vk7ZUsiXD4XJsQSjqYGIBw&usg=AFQjCNFVOoqN6STcvhZkghIpdwxRG7-mOQ&bvm=bv.59568121,d.cWc; Joseph Antos, "The Medicaid Expansion Is Not Such a Good Deal for States or the Poor," *Journal of*

Health Politics, Policy and Law 38, no. 1 (2013), 179–186, http://jhppl.dukejournals.org/content/early/2012/10/09/03616878-1898848.full.pdf.

8. Kaiser Commission, *The Medicaid Program at a Glance.*

9. Congressional Budget Office, *Medicaid—May 2013 Baseline.*

10. Kaiser Commission on Medicaid and the Uninsured, *Expanding Medicaid to Low-Income Childless Adults under Health Reform: Key Lessons from State Experiences*, July 1, 2010, http://kff.org/health-reform/issue-brief/expanding-medicaid-to-low-income-childless-adults/.

11. Using 133 or 138 percent of the federal poverty level (FPL) are both correct. The ACA expands Medicaid funding to cover adults under age 65 with income up to 133 percent of the FPL. For most people, the law also allows for up to 5 percent of income to be disregarded for eligibility purposes, which makes the effective rate 138 percent of the FPL.

12. Henry J. Kaiser Family Foundation, *A Guide to the Supreme Court's Decision on the ACA's Medicaid Expansion*, Menlo Park, CA, August 1, 2012, http://kff.org/health-reform/issue-brief/a-guide-to-the-supreme-courts-decision/.

13. This matching formula applies to the cost of most health services provided under Medicaid. There is a 50 percent match rate for administrative expenses, and a variety of adjustments are made for specific states, covered populations, types of service, emergency situations, and other circumstances. See Alison Mitchell and Evelyne P. Baumrucker, *Medicaid's Federal Medical Assistance Percentage (FMAP), FY2014*, R42941 (Washington, DC: Congressional Research Service, January 30, 2013), https://www.fas.org/sgp/crs/misc/R42941.pdf.

14. Vic Miller and Andy Schneider, *The Medicaid Matching Formula: Policy Considerations and Options for Modification* (Washington, DC: AARP, September 2004), http://www.aarp.org/health/medicare-insurance/info-2004/aresearch-import-918-2004-09.html.

15. Listed in descending order of federal payment. See Medicaid and CHIP Payment Access Commission, *Report to the Congress on Medicaid and CHIP* (Washington, DC: March 15, 2012), 98–99.

16. Mitchell and Baumrucker, *Medicaid's Federal Medical Assistance Percentage (FMAP), FY2014.* This report demonstrates that those states received a regular match rate of 50 percent every year, at least since 2006.

17. Kaiser Commission on Medicaid and the Uninsured, *Where Are States Today? Medicaid and CHIP Eligibility Levels for Children and Non-Disabled Adults*, March 28, 2013, http://kff.org/medicaid/fact-sheet/where-are-states-today-medicaid-and-chip/.

18. Listed in descending order of FMAP rate. See Henry J. Kaiser Family Foundation, *Federal Medical Assistance Percentage (FMAP) for Medicaid and Multiplier*, accessed June 2, 2013, http://kff.org/medicaid/state-indicator/federal-matching-rate-and-multiplier/.

19. US Treasury, *Historical Debt Outstanding—Annual*, 2000–2012, http://www.treasurydirect.gov/govt/reports/pd/histdebt/histdebt_histo5.htm.

20. National Association of State Budget Officers, Summary: NASBO *State Expenditure Report*, December 20, 2012, http://www.nasbo.org/sites/default/files/Summary%20-%20State%20Expenditure%20Report_0.pdf.

21. Rich Daly, "Expand and Contract," *Modern Healthcare*, March 8, 2013, http://www.modernhealthcare.com/article/20130308/MAGAZINE/303099955.

22. Vernon K. Smith et al., "Moving ahead Amid Fiscal Challenges: A Look at Medicaid Spending, Coverage and Policy Trends Results from a 50-State Medicaid Budget Survey for State Fiscal Years 2011 and 2012" (Menlo Park, CA: Henry J. Kaiser Family Foundation, October 1, 2011), http://kff.org/medicaid/report/moving-ahead-amid-fiscal-challenges-a-look-at-medicaid-spending-coverage-and-policy-trends-results-from-a-50-state-medicaid-budget-survey-for-state-fiscal-years-2011-and-2012/.

23. Ibid.

24. Phil Galewitz and Matthew Fleming, "13 States Cut Medicaid to Balance Budgets," *Kaiser Health News*, July 24, 2012, http://www.kaiserhealthnews.org/Stories/2012/July/25/medicaid-cuts.aspx.

25. Henry J. Kaiser Family Foundation, *Enhanced Medicaid Match Rates Expire in June 2011*, June 1, 2011, http://kff.org/health-reform/fact-sheet/enhanced-medicaid-match-rates-expire-in-june/.

26. National Association of State Budget Officers and the National Governors Association, *Fiscal Survey of States: Spring 2012*, Spring 2012, http://www.nasbo.org/publications-data/fiscal-survey-states/fiscal-survey-states-spring-2012.

27. Ibid.

28. See Medicaid.gov, *Managed Care*, accessed June 2, 2013, http://www.medicaid.gov/Medicaid-CHIP-Program-Information/By-Topics/Delivery-Systems/Managed-Care/Managed-Care.html.

29. Alison Mitchell, *Medicaid Financing and Expenditures*, R42640 (Washington, DC: Congressional Research Service, July 30, 2012), http://www.fas.org/sgp/crs/misc/R42640.pdf.

30. Andy Schneider and David Rousseau, "Medicaid Financing," in *The Medicaid Resource Book* (Menlo Park, CA: Henry J. Kaiser Family Foundation, July 2002), http://kff.org/medicaid/report/the-medicaid-resource-book/.

31. Alison Mitchell, *Medicaid Provider Taxes*, RS22843 (Washington, DC: Congressional Research Service, March 15, 2012), http://strategichealthcare.net/pdfs/45121463d.pdf.

32. Medicaid Voluntary Contributions and Provider-specific Tax Amendments, Pub. L. No. 102-234 (1991), http://www.google.com/url?sa=t&rct=j&q=&esrc=s&source=web&cd=2&ved=0CDQQFjAB&url=http%3A%2F%2Fwww.gpo.gov%2Ffdsys%2Fpkg%2FSTATUTE-105%2Fpdf%2FSTATUTE-105-Pg1793.pdf&ei=rV_ZUsiRB7PNsATAqoCgBQ&usg=AFQjCNFGU2BEhcYzJgHzAVWb2Fy6JENiUA&bvm=bv.59568121,d.cWc.

33. Henry J. Kaiser Family Foundation, *Quick Take: Medicaid Provider Taxes and Federal Deficit Reduction Efforts*, January 10, 2013, http://kff.org/medicaid/fact-sheet/medicaid-provider-taxes-and-federal-deficit-reduction-efforts-2/.

34. Kathryn Linehan, *Medicaid Financing: The Basics* (Washington, DC: National Health Policy Forum, February 13, 2013), http://www.nhpf.org/library/details.cfm/2528.

35. Mitchell, *Medicaid Provider Taxes*.

36. David Rousseau and Andy Schneider, *Current Issues in Medicaid Financing—An Overview of IGTs, UPLs, and DSH*, April 2004, http://kff.org/other/issue-brief/current-issues-in-medicaid-financing-an-overview/.

37. Ibid.

38. Robert E. Mechanic, *Medicaid's Disproportionate Share Hospital Program: Complex*

Structure, Critical Payments (Washington, DC: National Health Policy Forum, September 14, 2004), http://www.nhpf.org/library/background-papers/BP_MedicaidDSH_09-14-04.pdf.

39. Kathryn G. Allen, *Medicaid: Intergovernmental Transfers Have Facilitated State Financing Schemes*, GAO-04-574T (Washington, DC: Government Accountability Office, March 18, 2004), http://www.gao.gov/new.items/d04574t.pdf.
40. Rousseau and Schneider, *Current Issues in Medicaid Financing*.
41. Government Accountability Office, *Medicaid: More Transparency of and Accountability for Supplemental Payments Are Needed*, GAO-13-48 (Washington, DC: Government Accountability Office, November 26, 2012), http://www.gao.gov/products/GAO-13-48.
42. Author's calculation based on Teresa A. Coughlin, Brian K. Bruen, and Jennifer King, "States' Use of Medicaid UPL and DSH Financing Mechanisms," *Health Affairs* 23, no. 2 (2004): 245–257, http://content.healthaffairs.org/content/23/2/245.abstract.
43. Sara Rosenbaum, "Medicaid and Access to Health Care—A Proposal for Continued Inaction?," *New England Journal of Medicine* 365 (July 14, 2011): 102–4, http://www.nejm.org/doi/full/10.1056/NEJMp1106046.
44. Shatto and Clemens, "Projected Medicare Expenditures."
45. Jonathan Gruber and David Rodriguez, "How Much Uncompensated Care Do Doctors Provide?" (working paper 13585, National Bureau of Economic Research, Cambridge, MA, November 2007), http://www.nber.org/papers/w13585.
46. Peter J. Cunningham and Ann S. O'Malley, "Do Reimbursement Delays Discourage Medicaid Participation by Physicians?," *Health Affairs* 28, no. 1 (2009): w17–w28, http://content.healthaffairs.org/content/28/1/w17.abstract.
47. Ellyn R. Boukus, Alwyn Cassil, and Ann S. O'Malley, "A Snapshot of U.S. Physicians: Key Findings from the 2008 Health Tracking Physician Survey," Data Bulletin no. 35 (Washington, DC: Center for Studying Health System Change, September 2009), http://www.hschange.com/CONTENT/1078/1078.pdf.
48. Sandra L. Decker, "In 2011 Nearly One-Third of Physicians Said They Would Not Accept New Medicaid Patients, But Rising Fees May Help," *Health Affairs* 31, no. 8 (2012): 1673–79, http://content.healthaffairs.org/content/31/8/1673.abstract.
49. Joanna Bisgaier and Karin V. Rhodes, "Auditing Access to Specialty Care for Children with Public Insurance," *New England Journal of Medicine* 364, no. 24 (2011): 2324–33, http://www.nejm.org/doi/pdf/10.1056/NEJMsa1013285.
50. Boukus, Cassil, and O'Malley, "A Snapshot of U.S. Physicians."
51. Damien J. LaPar et al., "Primary Payer Status Affects Mortality for Major Surgical Operations," *Annals of Surgery* 252, no. 3 (2010): 544–51, http://www.ncbi.nlm.nih.gov/pmc/articles/PMC3071622/pdf/nihms279555.pdf.
52. Avik Roy, "The Medicaid Mess: How Obamacare Makes It Worse," No. 8 (New York: Manhattan Institute, March 2012), http://www.manhattan-institute.org/pdf/ir_8.pdf.
53. Paul Howard, "A Prescription for Medicaid," *National Affairs* no. 15 (2013): 51–70, http://www.nationalaffairs.com/publications/detail/a-prescription-for-medicaid.
54. Antos, "The Medicaid Expansion Is Not Such a Good Deal"; Kyle Cheney, "GOP Governors Name Their Price on Health Care Law Expansion," *Politico*, July 14, 2012, http://www.politico.com/news/stories/0712/78499.html.
55. Tom Suehs, "Human Services Chief: Why Medicaid Expansion Won't Work for Texas,"

American-Statesman, July 21, 2012, http://www.statesman.com/opinion/insight/human-services-chief-why-medicaid-expansion-wont-work-2420186.html.

56. Health Affairs, *Per Capita Caps in Medicaid*, Health Policy Brief, April 18, 2013, http://www.healthaffairs.org/healthpolicybriefs/brief.php?brief_id=90; David Sutter, "Welfare Block Grants as a Guide for Medicaid Reform" (Working Paper 13-07, Mercatus Center, Arlington, VA, March 2013), http://mercatus.org/publication/welfare-block-grants-guide-medicaid-reform.

57. For example, see Fred Upton and Orrin Hatch, *Making Medicaid Work*, May 1, 2013, http://energycommerce.house.gov/sites/republicans.energycommerce.house.gov/files/analysis/20130501Medicaid.pdf.

58. Estimate is average enrollment over the course of a year, not the number of individuals who had at least one month of Medicaid enrollment. In 2013, for example, CBO estimates that average annual enrollment in Medicaid and CHIP is 36 million. The number of people enrolled at any point during the fiscal year is estimated to be 71 million for Medicaid and 8.4 million for CHIP. See Congressional Budget Office, *Effects on Health Insurance and the Federal Budget for the Insurance Coverage Provisions in the Affordable Care Act—May 2013 Baseline*, May 14, 2013, http://www.cbo.gov/publication/44190; Congressional Budget Office, *Medicaid—May 2013 Baseline*, May 14, 2013, http://www.cbo.gov/publication/44204; and Congressional Budget Office, *Children's Health Insurance Program—* May 2013 *Baseline*, May 14, 2013, http://www.cbo.gov/publication/44189.

CHAPTER 2: MEDICAID'S COST DRIVERS

JUNE O'NEILL

Medicaid is the primary source of health care funding for America's low-income population. The program is now very large by most any standard. In 2012, 68 million people were enrolled in Medicaid at some point during the year.[1] The program now serves a larger population than Medicare. Medicaid is state based and administered, but is jointly funded by the general revenues of the federal government and the states. In fiscal year (FY) 2011, total Medicaid expenditures were $432 billion, 64 percent of which was funded by the federal government and 36 percent by the states. Each of the 50 states administers its own Medicaid program subject to federal requirements concerning such matters as program eligibility and the treatment of beneficiaries and medical providers. But the states have little incentive to reduce costs because under the federal matching program they lose federal dollars for every program dollar saved. Given the complex federal-state funding structure and conflicting state incentives, the federal government faces a daunting problem.

Rapid growth has characterized both Medicaid expenditures and Medicaid beneficiaries (figures 1 and 2). Medicaid is an important contributor to the rise of total spending on health care in the United

Figure 1. Total Medicaid Payments, Fiscal Years 1975–2010

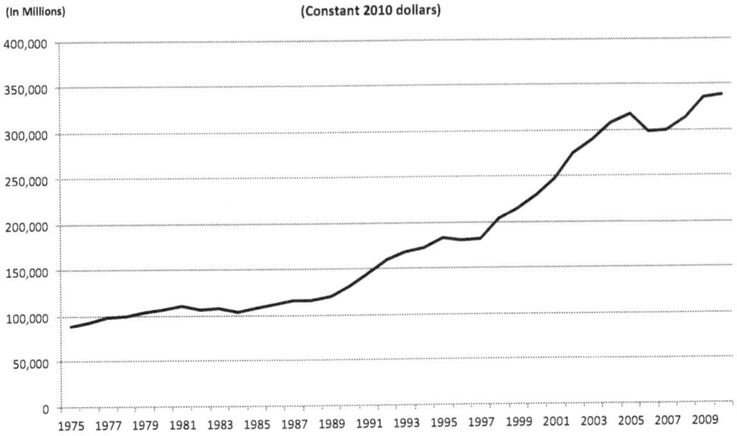

(In Millions)
(Constant 2010 dollars)
400,000
350,000
300,000
250,000
200,000
150,000
100,000
50,000
0
1975 1977 1979 1981 1983 1985 1987 1989 1991 1993 1995 1997 1999 2001 2003 2005 2007 2009

Source: Medicare and Medicaid Research Review, *2012 Statistical Supplement, Table 13.10.*

Figure 2. Number of Medicaid Beneficiaries, Fiscal Years 1975–2010

(In Thousands)
70,000
60,000
50,000
40,000
30,000
20,000
10,000
0
1975 1977 1979 1981 1983 1985 1987 1989 1991 1993 1995 1997 1999 2001 2003 2005 2007 2009

Source: Medicare and Medicaid Research Review, *2012 Statistical Supplement, Table 13.4.*

States, which now consumes 17.7 percent of gross domestic product (GDP). National health expenditures (NHE), a global measure covering all health spending, both privately and publicly funded, rose from 12.5 percent of GDP in 1990 to 17.7 percent in 2011. Over the

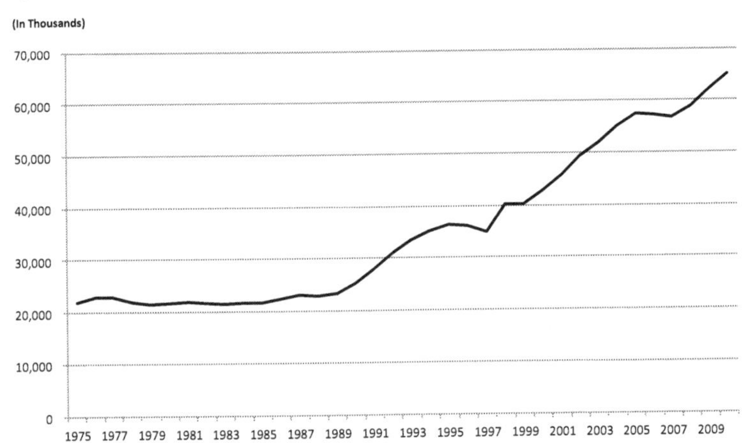

same period, spending on Medicaid increased as a share of NHE, from 10 percent of NHE to 15 percent. Measured as a percent of GDP, Medicaid rose from 1.0 percent of GDP in 1985 to 2.9 percent in 2011.

The growth in Medicaid expenditures over time has been spurred by increases in the size of the population groups eligible for program participation as well as by increases in the cost of delivering medical care to those groups. Program costs are also affected by changes in the broader economy, such as economic fluctuations and changes in provider prices. Additionally, program costs are affected by programmatic changes such as those in the federal share of total expenditures and in federal guidelines setting terms of eligibility, as well as changes in state policies concerning covered services. Fraud and abuse have also plagued both Medicare and Medicaid. A recent study estimated that fraud and abuse in the two programs cost the federal government as much as $98 billion in 2011.[2] Efforts by states to enlarge federal Medicaid payments have also been legally questionable at times.[3]

The Patient Protection and Affordable Care Act (ACA) is likely to have a significant effect on the Medicaid program.[4] As originally passed, the ACA mandated that state Medicaid programs cover all individuals with incomes below 133 percent of the federal poverty level (FPL).[5] This provision would extend Medicaid to those who were not previously eligible for the program because their incomes were too high. (The previous income limit had been set at the FPL.) In addition, the expansion would extend coverage to single adults without children, a group that had been excluded from Medicaid. The expansion was scheduled to start in 2014 and was estimated to add 17 million nonelderly adults to the Medicaid rolls by 2022. In 2012, however, the Supreme Court held that the mandate requiring the state expansion of Medicaid was unconstitutionally coercive.[6]

As a result of the Supreme Court decision, it is now optional for states to decide whether or not to proceed with the expansion. To induce states to sign on to the expansion, the federal government agreed to pay 100 percent of hospital and other medical bills of the newly covered beneficiaries for a period of three years. After that, the federal payment is scheduled to drop to 90 percent. (For a detailed description of how the ACA will affect Medicaid in the states, see chapter 5, page 65.)

It is difficult to predict the long-run impact of the expansion on Medicaid costs. For example, if those who enter the program initially are adults who turn out to have expensive chronic conditions, cost pressure might very well rise. The states appear to be conflicted. As of July 1, 2013, 24 states indicated that they are moving forward with the expansion, 21 indicated that they are not moving forward, and 6 said that debate in their state was ongoing.[7]

PROGRAM HISTORY AND DETAILS

Medicaid became law in 1965 under Title XIX of the Social Security Act. The program was created to provide funds for medical services to low-income groups. In addition to income and asset limitations, eligibility for federal funds was tied primarily to receipt of public welfare assistance in what was then Aid to Families with Dependent Children (AFDC), and to the low-income elderly, blind, and disabled groups who receive Supplemental Security Income (SSI). Although AFDC in 1996 was replaced by Temporary Assistance for Needy Families (TANF), eligibility for Medicaid is still automatic for low-income families with children who meet the requirements for AFDC as specified in 1996. Medicaid eligibility is also extended to those low-income elderly and disabled who qualify for SSI.

Although federal law requires states to cover certain population groups and sets certain financial eligibility criteria, states can apply for waivers to expand coverage beyond the specified groups. A state can also cover certain groups without federal approval if it is willing to fully pay the costs of the group without federal assistance. Within the federal guidelines, each state establishes its own eligibility standards, determines the amount and duration of services offered, sets the rate of payment for services, and generally administers its own program.

States vary considerably with respect to the relative size of their low-income populations and population characteristics, such as the proportion with chronic problems that would allow classification as disabled. Not surprisingly, program participation and costs per enrollee differ considerably across the states. Thus in FY2009, the average share of a state's population enrolled in Medicaid was 20 percent. In California, however, 30 percent of residents were enrolled; in Utah only 6 percent were enrolled. The average Medicaid payment per beneficiary in the United States in 2009 was $5,527. The highest per capita payment was in Connecticut ($9,577); the lowest in Georgia ($3,979).[8] Connecticut's high payment is attributable to a relatively large proportion of their beneficiary population qualifying for long-term care.

As Joseph Antos explains in chapter 1, the federal government pays a share of the expenditures in each state's Medicaid program. That share, known as the federal medical assistance percentage (FMAP), is determined annually by a formula based on the state's per capita income compared with the national average income. The federal share is larger in states with lower per capita income. The FMAP by law can be no lower than 50 percent or higher than 83 percent. The historical average has been a 57 percent state share. However, the American Recovery and Reinvestment Act (ARRA) of 2009, enacted as part of an effort to stimulate recovery from the 2008 financial crisis, gave states a temporary increase in their FMAPs of up to 14 percentage points, depending on their unemployment rates. The FMAP boost was in place from the first quarter of FY2009 through the first quarter of FY2011. Additional legislation continued the higher rates through the second and third quarters of 2011, but at lower levels. In FY2013, the FMAP ranged from a low of 50 percent (12 states including New York, New Jersey, and California) to a high of 73.4 percent in Mississippi.

The dramatic shifts in Medicaid funding during the recession are displayed in table 1 along with information on changes in annual growth rates in total health spending (NHE) as well as in other major sources of health care funding, public and private. For each spending

Table 1. Growth in National Health Expenditures (NHE) and in Selected Spending Sources, Percentage Change from Previous Year (calendar years 1990–2011)

	1990	2000	2007	2008	2009	2010	2011
NHE	11.0	6.6	6.2	4.7	3.9	3.9	3.9
Medicaid	11.0	10.5	6.3	5.8	8.8	5.9	2.5
Federal	11.4	10.6	6.7	9.6	21.9	7.7	-7.1
State	10.4	10.4	5.7	0.7	–10.0	2.5	22.2
Medicare	11.4	7.4	7.4	8.0	6.9	4.3	6.2
Private Health Insurance	13.0	7.0	5.0	3.9	3.2	3.4	3.8
Out-of-Pocket	9.0	3.8	5.3	2.4	0.1	2.1	2.8
GDP	5.8	6.4	4.9	1.9	–2.2	3.9	4.0
Real GDP*	1.9	4.1	1.9	–0.3	–3.1	2.4	1.9

** Chained 2005 dollars (Department of Commerce, BEA).*
Source: NHE and the component health expenditures are from Centers for Medicare and Medicaid Services, Office of the National Health Statistics Group.

source, the table shows the percentage change in expenditures from the previous year. As shown, growth rates in health care spending had generally been high in 1990 when Medicaid expenditures increased at an annual rate of 11 percent—the same as the growth rate in NHE. By 2000, Medicaid growth was still at the high level of 1990 although spending was reduced in most other sources of health care funding. But during the following decade, the slowdown in GDP growth was reflected in lower spending on health care expenditures generally, including Medicaid expenditures. Thus, Medicaid spending, federal and state combined, increased by 5.8 percent in 2008 from the previous year.[9] With the advent of the recession, federal spending accounted for most of that increase as the state share barely increased at all (a rise of 0.3 percent).

Once the full impact of the recession hit in 2009, the annual percentage increase in total Medicaid expenditures rose to 8.8 percent, more than double the rate of increase in NHE. High unemployment led to additional enrollments and higher Medicaid costs. At the same time, states were financially stressed by plunging revenues related to the high unemployment. As a consequence, state Medicaid spending actually fell by 10 percent. But as part of the recession stimulus effort, the federal government came to the rescue with close to a 22 percent increase in federal funds, which more than offset the collapse in state funding.

The funding of Medicaid differs considerably from that of Medicare in that it is almost entirely drawn from general revenues—both state and federal—whereas Medicare is substantially funded by dedicated revenue sources: payroll taxes and beneficiary premiums. Medicaid is therefore highly important in state budgets. According to the National Association of State Budget Officers (NASBO), in FY2012, Medicaid accounted for 23.9 percent of all state government spending. That percentage exceeded the spending share of all other programs, including elementary and secondary school spending, which accounted for 19.8 percent.[10] (For further details on the impact of Medicaid on federal and state budgets, see chapters 3 and 4, pages 49 and 65.)

SOURCES OF RISING COSTS

Since its inception in 1966, the spending trajectory of the Medicaid program has been upward, although the rate of increase has varied, sometimes considerably (see figure 1). Medicaid expenditures are driven by growth both in enrollments of beneficiaries (figure 2) and in the medical costs incurred by the beneficiaries.

Costs per beneficiary vary considerably with the characteristics of beneficiaries. Those who are elderly or disabled incur much higher medical costs than children or nonelderly adults; thus, changes in the composition of beneficiaries have a significant effect on costs. The economy influences the flow of beneficiaries, particularly those in the child and nonelderly adult category because increases and decreases in employment affect income eligibility for the program (e.g., family income for children; own income for nonelderly single adults).

Table 2. Distribution of Medicaid Recipients and Medicaid Payments by Eligibility Group and Medicaid Payments per Person Served by Eligibility Group, 1990, 2000, 2010

	Share of Beneficiaries (%)			Share of Payments (%)			Per Person Served* ($)		
	1990	2000	2010	1990	2000	2010	1990	2000	2010
Children	44.7	46.1	48.4	14.0	15.9	19.9	1,642	1,853	2,129
Adult	23.8	20.5	23.9	13.2	10.6	12.8	2,893	2,771	3,102
Aged	13.7	8.7	6.6	33.2	26.4	19.4	13,597	16,282	15,339
Disabled	14.7	16.1	14.3	37.6	43.2	43.5	13,282	14,413	15,752
Other/ Unknown	3.1	8.6	6.8	2.0	3.9	4.4			
Total	100	100	100	100	100	100			

* *Constant 2010 dollars.*
Source: Data are from the Medicare and Medicaid Research Review, 2012, Statistical Supplement.

Medicaid also at times has been affected by episodes such as the explosion in costs generated by the Medicaid disproportionate share hospital (DSH) program, described below.

The relation between demographic characteristics, per enrollee costs, and total payments is shown in table 2 for the years 1990, 2000, and 2010. Medicaid enrollees are usually identified as belonging to one of four major demographic groups: children, adult, elderly, and disabled. Enrollees classified as adults in the Medicaid program are nondisabled and younger than age 65. As table 2 indicates, Medicaid payments per capita differ considerably by characteristic. In all years shown, children and adults are the lowest cost recipients. In 2010, Medicaid payments per beneficiary were $2,129 for children and $3,102 for the adult category. By contrast, payment per beneficiary was $15,339 for the elderly and $15,752 for the disabled.

The total number of beneficiaries increased from 25 million to 65 million between 1990 and 2010—a rise of 158 percent. Changes in the demographic composition of beneficiaries did not play a major role in the increase in costs over that period. The number of children beneficiaries increased as a percentage of the total and was the only one of the four groups to do so. The increase, however, was modest. Over the 20-year period, the children's share of the beneficiary population grew from 45 percent to 48 percent.

But cost pressures did rise for the children group because per person costs increased more for children than the other groups—a 30 percent rise in real dollars between 1990 and 2010. Children remained the lowest per capita payment group in 2010, although the combination of a small gain in beneficiary share and a significant increase in per person payments increased the children's share of total payments from 14 to 20 percent. The adult group retained their share of about 24 percent of total beneficiaries. They, like children, are a relatively low cost group. In 2010, they accounted for a somewhat smaller share of total payments than was the case in 1990.

Unlike the pattern for the other groups, the Medicaid participation of the elderly declined significantly over the 20-year period, falling from a share of 13.7 percent of total beneficiaries in 1990 to only 6.8 percent in 2010. The elderly are a high-cost group; but as their participation declined, their share of total Medicaid payments fell from 33 percent in 1990 to 19 percent in 2010. Disabled beneficiaries are the other high-cost group. As shown in table 2, the per capita payments of the disabled are quite similar to those of the elderly. But unlike the elderly, the disabled have remained a fairly steady share of total beneficiaries, at about 14 percent. But because their per person payments are high and have been rising—an increase of 18.5 percent in constant dollars between 1990 and 2010—their share of total Medicaid payments has increased from 38 percent in 1990 to 44 percent in 2010, the largest percentage share of any group.

Medicaid is often viewed as an important funding mechanism for long-term medical care in nursing homes. Nursing homes are not exclusively used by low-income people. Middle class individuals may enter nursing homes as paying residents. But nursing home care is expensive and residents who exhaust their financial assets become dependent on Medicaid to pay the bills. In 2010, the average payment per elderly Medicaid recipient for nursing home care was about

$35,000. Only 2.4 percent of the total Medicaid population used nursing home facilities in 2010. But even among elderly recipients, use of nursing facilities has declined significantly. In 1990, 39.5 percent of elderly Medicaid recipients were counted as users of nursing facilities; by 2010, that percentage had fallen to 24.3. Nursing homes are the second most heavily used service by the elderly in Medicaid. Prescribed drugs are the most heavily used: 45 percent of elderly recipients receive drug benefits. But the percentage receiving drug benefits has declined sharply as Medicaid recipients who are also Medicare recipients (so-called dual eligibles) have been shifted into Medicare Part D.

The pattern of nursing home usage in Medicaid is consistent with data released from the Bureau of the Census indicating that the percentage of Americans ages 75 and older living in nursing homes fell from 10.2 percent in 1990 to 5.7 percent in 2010. Among those ages 85 and older, the percentage in nursing homes fell from 21.6 percent in 1985 to 11.6 percent in 2010.[11] Assisted living arrangements and other community services that enable people to stay in the community are replacing nursing homes.

Such alternatives to nursing homes have become more viable because the income and wealth of the elderly have increased. It is often assumed that the elderly play a significant role in rising health care costs because medical problems increase with age. Although that is true, it is also true that because of gains in medical science and technology, many of the infirmities of old age have been alleviated by such procedures as knee and hip replacements, which enable people to remain more self-sufficient at advanced ages. The older population today has increased its labor force participation and economic status. Successive generations in the United States have become more educated and have attained higher earnings. Recent studies find that the assets of the elderly have increased considerably over time.[12] The increase in resources of the elderly helps explain the declining importance of this demographic in the Medicaid program.

Individuals with disabilities account for 14 percent of Medicaid recipients, and that proportion has been relatively stable for many years.

Many of the disabled who qualify for Medicaid also receive cash benefits from the SSI program. In most states SSI eligibility automatically qualifies an individual for Medicaid. In the other states, applicants must demonstrate that they have an impairment that prevents them from working for at least one year. In addition, applicants must pass a review of assets and income before they qualify for Medicaid. Included in the Medicaid disabled group are individuals with HIV/AIDS, for whom Medicaid is the single largest source of coverage. Although the number of beneficiaries with HIV is growing, coverage for this group still represents less than 3 percent of Medicaid spending.[13] Medicaid data on the services used by the disabled indicate that provision of prescribed drugs and physician services are the most heavily used.

THE DSH EPISODE

It is not surprising that in a program as large as Medicaid, with two major sources of funding, difficulties regarding cost control and instances of fraudulent practices would arise. The most notorious example of the latter involves the Medicaid DSH program, which in the early 1990s was responsible for several years of huge cost increases in federal Medicaid expenditures.[14]

The DSH program involves hospitals that serve a disproportionate number of low-income and uninsured people, and as a consequence have difficulty getting their bills paid. In the early 1980s, Congress attempted to alleviate the problem by mandating that states consider making special payments to disproportionate share hospitals. Few states responded. Congress then added the stipulation that the disproportionate share hospitals could bill the states using the higher reimbursement rates of Medicare.

To help states raise funds to reimburse the hospitals, CMS, at that time called the Health Care Financing Administration, issued a rule that allowed states to receive donations from medical providers. This was an attractive option for states; when they ran out of funds during times of hardship, they were unable to pay providers and therefore could not apply for any federal matching money. The donations rule enabled hospitals to make a donation to the state. The state then pays the hospital with the donation money and that payment generates an expenditure that qualifies the state to obtain matching payments from the federal government. The state gains the federal money even though little, if any, of the federal payment actually goes to the hospital. The states embellished the idea by adopting provider tax programs that operated similar to the donations. And the payments back to the hospitals were labeled as DSH payments. With the donation and tax schemes, the states were able to leverage the DSH payments into considerable state funds that partly helped the hospitals and partly could be used for other state purposes.

The period of peak DSH activity was 1990–92. In 1992, DSH spending accounted for significant amounts of spending in many states; for example, it accounted for 43 percent of Louisiana's spending.[15] Medicaid spending in the federal budget escalated, recording annual increases of as much as 30 percent in a single year.

The rapid rise of federal DSH payments did not go unnoticed. Legislation to deal with the problem began in 1991 with the Medicaid Voluntary Contribution and Provider-Specific Tax Amendments (the legislation arose from an agreement between the administration of President George H. W. Bush and the National Governor's Association). The agreement set caps on DSH payments, limiting them to 12 percent of total Medicaid costs. Provider donations were banned and provider taxes were restricted.

But the DSH problem was not fully resolved. States soon developed a new means of raising money for their DSH programs. Money within state budgets is frequently fungible, and many states turned to intergovernmental transfers (IGT) to transfer money from one agency or level of government to another. Thus, some states transferred funds from public institutions such as state psychiatric facilities, state university hospitals, and other public hospitals (city, county) to the state Medicaid agency. The state could then make DSH payments to these public hospitals, once again generating federal share payments. By 1992, DSH accounted for 15.4 percent of total Medicaid spending. Accounts surfaced that DSH payments were not being used for their stated purpose, but instead were retained by states for general state funding.[16]

Congress eventually cut back spending on the DSH program through provisions included in the 1993 Omnibus Budget Reconciliation Agreement and the Balanced Budget Act of 1997.

DUAL ELIGIBLES

On another front, the federal government and states are facing the escalating costs of covering the group of elderly and disabled individuals who are jointly enrolled in Medicare and Medicaid. Funding and eligibility for the two programs differs, as does the provision of benefits. People who are eligible for the two programs at the same time are called "dual-eligible beneficiaries." "Full-duals" are eligible for full benefits from both programs. "Partial duals" qualify for Medicare but do not meet the eligibility requirement for all Medicaid benefits. In 2009, dual eligibles made up 13 percent of the combined population of Medicare enrollees and elderly, blind, and disabled Medicaid enrollees. But they accounted for 34 percent of the two programs' total spending on those enrollees.[17]

CONCLUDING COMMENTS

The provision of health care in the United States is a patchwork. Employer-based coverage started during World War II as wage controls prevented firms from raising workers' wages. Fringe benefits, most particularly health insurance, were exempt from the controls. It was believed that eventually most workers and their families would gain coverage through their employers. As life expectancy rose, concerns about the retired population led to the development of Medicare. Medicaid was added to fill the gap for people who depended on public assistance and therefore lacked employer-based insurance or Medicare.

Medicaid now covers medical care for one-fifth of the US population. The expansion of Medicaid, spurred by the ACA, would further enlarge the program in those states that sign on to the expansion. It is difficult to control costs and provide incentives for efficiency when jurisdiction and funding are shared. Federal contributions to the states are difficult to direct and control because the payments are fungible. The DSH problem arose for that reason. If the federal payments for the ACA expansion are limited to direct payment of medical bills rather than contributions to the states to pay the bills, the potential for cost escalation may be limited. Medicaid is a unique program. It is state administered, involving 50 states each with different demographic characteristics and income levels. The funding mechanism is complex because it is jointly funded by the federal government and the states, with the federal government paying 57 percent of the total. States have a blunted incentive to reduce spending because they lose federal money for every program dollar saved. Medicaid is clearly a challenge to lawmakers who are responsible for the program.

One alternative that has been periodically considered as a way to provide medical care more efficiently to the low-income population is the mechanism of block grants. The welfare reform of the 1990s essentially converted the old AFDC program into block grants for funding and this has proven to be successful. Presumably, under a block grant, Medicaid still would be required to meet appropriate standards of medical care. The particular mode of administering services would be up to the states, which would likely have different approaches tailored to the characteristics of their populations. But the big difference would be that states would have to deal with a monetary ceiling on federal funds, which presumably would spur cost containment.

NOTES

1. Some people are enrolled for only part of the year. Taking that fact into account, the Congressional Budget Office (CBO) estimates that enrollment over the course of FY2012 was 55 million expressed as full-year equivalents.
2. Donald M. Berwick and Andrew D. Hackbarth, "Eliminating Waste in US Health Care," *Journal of the American Medical Association* 307, no. 14 (2012): 1513–6, doi:10.1001/jama.2012.362.
3. See the discussion of the DSH episode below.
4. Patient Protection and Affordable Care Act, Pub. L. No. 111-148, 124 Stat. 119 (2010) (codified as amended sections of 42 U.S.C.).
5. The effective new income limit is 138 percent of the FPL, since in addition to raising the income level to 133 percent, 5 percent of income is disregarded.
6. On June 28, 2012, the US Supreme Court issued its decision in the case challenging the constitutionality of the ACA, National Federation of Independent Business (NFIB) v. Sebelius 132 S. Ct. 2566.
7. These tabulations are from the Henry J. Kaiser Family Foundation, "State Health Facts: Status of State Action on Medicaid Expansion decision as of July 1, 2013."
8. The data on state enrollment and payment rates are from the Kaiser Commission on Medicaid and the Uninsured.
9. Note that the percentage change for all years shown is the percentage change from the previous year.
10. For data on state spending see Summary: NASBO Report on State Expenditures, December 20, 2012.
11. Data for 2010 are reported in US Census Bureau, 2010 Census Summary File 1. Data for 1990 were reported in a US Census Bureau, Census 2000 Special tabulation and 1990 Census of Population Report, nursing home population: 1990 (CPH-L-1371). A special census report of September 27, 2007, also noted the decline in nursing home use among the elderly that was reported widely in the *Wall Street Journal, USA Today*, and other news briefs.
12. See for example, Bricker, Kennickell, Moore, and Sabelhaus, "Changing U.S. Family Finances from 2007 to 2010: Evidence from the Survey of Consumer Finances," *Federal Reserve Bulletin* (2012). They find striking change in the age distribution of net worth. The most recent data show that the age group 75 years of age and older now has the highest median net worth.
13. See Henry J. Kaiser Family Foundation, "Medicaid and HIV/AIDS," March 5, 2013.
14. For further discussion of the DSH program, see Theresa A Coughlin and David Liska, *The Medicaid Disproportionate Share Hospital Payment Program: Background and Issues*, Series A No. A-14 (Urban Institute, October 1997).
15. Ibid.
16. L. Se Ku and T. A. Coughlin, "Medicaid Disproportionate Share and Other Special Financing Programs," *Health Care Financing Review* 16, no. 3 (1995).
17. See Congressional Budget Office, "Dual-Eligible Beneficiaries of Medicare and Medicaid: Characteristics, Health Care Spending and Evolving Policies" (Congressional Budget Office, June 2013).

PART 2:

MEDICAID'S BUDGETARY IMPACT

CHAPTER 3: THE FEDERAL SIDE OF THE BUDGET EQUATION

JASON J. FICHTNER

Often called an afterthought to the Medicare program, Medicaid was signed into law under Title XIX of the Social Security Act. Unlike Medicare, which was created to provide health care coverage to those over the age of 65, Medicaid's intent was the provision of care for individuals of any age whose incomes were limited. In 1966, Medicaid provided health insurance to 10 million beneficiaries.[1] Currently, with approximately 57 million people enrolled, and about 69 million people enrolled at some point during 2013, Medicaid has evolved into the largest health insurance provider in the United States.[2]

Federal Medicaid costs are expected to increase dramatically. The Congressional Budget Office (CBO) estimates that by 2024, 20 million new people will be added to Medicaid (and the Children's Health Insurance Program) under the Patient Protection and Affordable Care Act (ACA)[3]—an increase of nearly 30 percent.[4] Further, according to CBO, federal spending on Medicaid is already projected to rapidly increase under the ACA, rising from $265 billion in fiscal year (FY) 2013 to $574 billion in FY2024.[5] As will be discussed later in the chapter, any estimate of the federal government's future cost obligations are also dependent on how many states, and which states, choose to expand their state Medicaid program. Also of financial concern, at the time of writing this chapter, early indications in implementation of the ACA show that many more people than previously estimated are logging onto healthcare.gov and signing up for Medicaid, possibly expanding Medicaid participation and costs beyond their original estimates.[6]

WHAT IS MEDICAID?

Medicaid is a government health insurance program providing coverage to individuals who are limited in their ability to financially afford medical care.[7] The program is run by each individual state with major funding assistance from federal cost-sharing dollars. Though state participation in Medicaid is voluntary, all 50 states and the District of Columbia participate. Each state, using federal matching funds, establishes and administers its own Medicaid program. As long as a state follows federal guidelines, it has the flexibility to determine the type and scope of services provided.[8] Additionally, each state has the option of charging enrollees' premiums and establishing out-of-pocket spending requirements such as copayments, coinsurance, and deductibles.

Although Medicaid eligibility varies dramatically from state to state, in order to qualify for federal funding, each state must provide coverage to limited-income families with children as well as individuals who are elderly, blind, or disabled (see the percentage breakdown in figure 1).[9] (See chapter 2, page 37, for an explanation of the demographic changes of Medicaid beneficiaries over time.)

Though states impose their own income thresholds, an individual or family applying for Medicaid cannot exceed a certain income threshold, which is calculated in relation to a percentage of the federal poverty level (FPL). Today, the FPL ranges from $11,490 for a family of one to $39,630 for a family of eight.[10] For example, consider a pregnant woman comprising a family of one and fitting categorically into

Figure 1. FY2013 Medicaid Enrollees

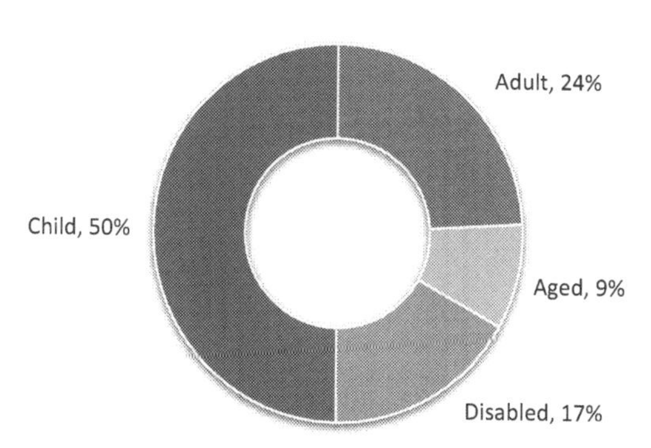

Source: Centers for Medicare & Medicaid Services, CMS Financial Report, Fiscal Year 2013 *(Baltimore, MD: Department of Health & Human Services, 2013), http://www.cms.gov/Research-Statistics-Data-and-Systems/Statistics-Trends-and-Reports/CFOReport/Downloads/2013_CMS_Financial_Report.pdf.*

one of Medicaid's mandatory eligibility groups. In 2013, the median Medicaid threshold (across 50 states and the District of Columbia) for this individual was 185 percent of the FPL.[11] This would make her eligible for Medicaid if she earned less than $21,257.

It is important to note that states may offer a greater number and additional types of services above and beyond what is mandated by the Department of Health and Human Services (HHS). Through Section 1115 of the Social Security Act, the federal government has encouraged states to tailor the Medicaid program to their unique political and economic environments.[12] Building on Section 1115, the Health Insurance Flexibility and Accountability (HIFA) demonstration initiative gives states enhanced "waiver flexibility to streamline benefits packages, create public-private partnerships, and increase cost-sharing for optional and expansion populations covered under Medicaid."[13] Contingent on approval by the HHS secretary, state leaders are empowered to develop a unique program that meets the needs of their individual state.[14] Because of the federal matching formula, how each state determines, and ultimately designs, its state Medicaid program directly impacts the federal government's spending on Medicaid.

HOW MEDICAID IS FUNDED

As Antos explains in chapter 1 (page 9), Medicaid is a matching-grant program jointly funded by federal and state governments. To determine the share of Medicaid the federal government will pay in each state, the HHS calculates the federal medical assistance percentage (FMAP):[15]

$$\text{FMAP} = 100\% - \left[\frac{(\text{State per capita income})^2}{(\text{US per capita income})^2} \times 0.45\right]$$

Instituted in 1965, the FMAP formula ensures that the federal government pays a higher proportion of Medicaid costs in states where the average income per capita is lower relative to the national average. Using income data averaged over three years, the HHS provides an updated FMAP value every fiscal year between October 1 and November 30. For purposes of this formula, "income" represents personal income as calculated by the Bureau of Economic Analysis instead of money income as calculated by the Census Bureau. To control the amount paid by either the federal or state government, threshold limits bind the FMAP between 50 and 83 percent.[16] FMAPs as of FY2013 are shown in table 1.

THE PATIENT PROTECTION AND AFFORDABLE CARE ACT

In an attempt to increase the number of Medicaid recipients, the ACA as it was originally written created a new category of individuals eligible for Medicaid. Without noting the specific caveats, this category extended coverage to all individuals whose incomes fell below 133 percent of the FPL (accounting for a 5 percent federal income exclusion, this threshold effectively increases to 138 percent of the FPL) who were not previously eligible for Medicaid.[17] Based on an estimate from the Centers for Medicare and Medicaid Services (CMS), this coverage expansion was estimated to increase total projected Medicaid enrollment by 14.9 million people in 2014 and 25.9 million people by 2020.[18]

Table 1. Federal Medical Assistance Percentages, FY2013

State	FMAP (%)	State	FMAP (%)	State	FMAP (%)
Alabama	68.53	Kentucky	70.55	North Dakota	52.27
Alaska	50.00	Louisiana	61.24	Ohio	63.58
Arizona	65.68	Maine	62.57	Oklahoma	64.00
Arkansas	70.71	Maryland	50.00	Oregon	62.44
California	50.00	Massachusetts	50.00	Pennsylvania	54.28
Colorado	50.00	Michigan	66.39	Rhode Island	51.26
Connecticut	50.00	Minnesota	50.00	South Carolina	70.43
Delaware	55.67	Mississippi	73.43	South Dakota	56.19
District of Columbia*	70.00	Missouri	61.37	Tennessee	66.13
Florida	58.08	Montana	66.00	Texas	59.30
Georgia	65.56	Nebraska	55.76	Utah	69.61
Hawaii	51.86	Nevada	59.74	Vermont	56.04
Idaho	71.00	New Hampshire	50.00	Virginia	50.00
Illinois	50.00	New Jersey	50.00	Washington	50.00
Indiana	67.16	New Mexico	69.07	West Virginia	72.04
Iowa	59.59	New York	50.00	Wisconsin	59.74
Kansas	56.51	North Carolina	65.51	Wyoming	50.00

** The values for the District of Columbia in the table were set for the state plan under Titles XIX and XXI and for capitation payments and disproportionate share hospital allotments under those titles. For other purposes, the percentage for the District of Columbia is 50.00, unless otherwise specified by law.*
Source: 76 Fed. Reg 74061-74063 (Nov. 30, 2011).

Under current law, the HHS secretary is permitted to withhold federal funding if a state fails to comply with the minimum benefit and eligibility requirements established by the federal government. Originally, the ACA stipulated that states that failed to expand their Medicaid coverage would be considered noncompliant. In its review of the ACA's constitutionality, the Supreme Court held that the Medicaid expansion clause in the ACA was unconstitutionally coercive.[19] Chief Justice John Roberts's opinion held that the mandatory expansion of Medicaid coupled with the HHS secretary's authority to withhold funding for noncompliance is a "gun to the head" because the "threatened loss of 10 percent of a State's overall budget is economic dragooning that leaves the States with no real option but to acquiesce."[20] To allow the provisions set forth in the ACA to remain intact while providing a remedy for the coercion inherent in the act, the Supreme Court precluded the HHS secretary's ability to withhold existing Medicaid funds for failing to comply with the Medicaid expansion requirements, leaving only the incentive of increased funding to encourage states to expand Medicaid eligibility.[21] For newly eligible individuals, the federal government will pay 100 percent of the costs for the first three years. Starting in 2017, the percentage paid is supposed to decrease and ultimately settle at 90 percent in 2020.[22]

MEDICAID AND THE COST IMPLICATIONS OF THE ACA

The Supreme Court's ruling effectively relegates the choice to expand Medicaid to the states. Hence, any estimate of the federal government's future cost obligations now necessarily depend on how many states, and which states, choose to expand their Medicaid program. From a state's perspective, the decision to expand coverage depends on two competing values. Charles Blahous, a public trustee for Social Security and Medicare, recently analyzed the incentives facing states under the ACA. He finds that a state governor faces an incentive to "maximize the health benefits his own state's citizens receive that are financed by entities outside of the state, while also minimizing his state's budgetary exposure."[23] He elaborates on the ACA's impact on state budgets in chapter 5 (page 86).

The decision to expand coverage is complex for state policymakers. Though the federal government agreed to cover a significant portion of associated expenses in order to influence states to expand Medicaid, each state must project how the Medicaid expansion will affect its current and future budgets. Considering Medicaid represented less than 3 percent of total state and local expenditures in 1967, whereas in FY2012 it represents an estimated 24 percent of total expenditures,

Figure 2. Projected Medicaid Expenditures

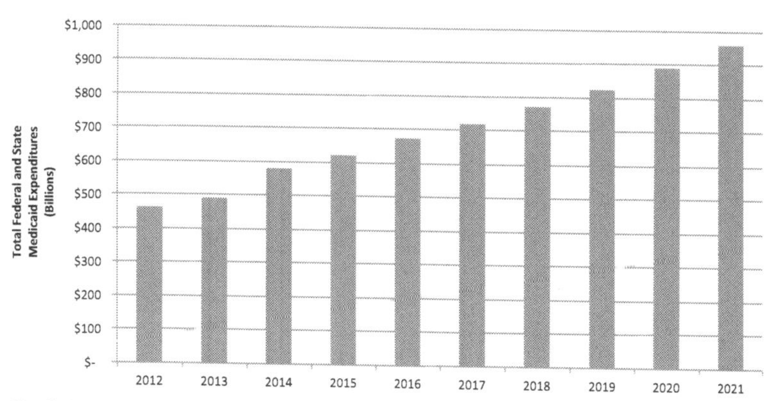

Note: Projections assume universal participation.
Source: Centers for Medicare & Medicaid Services, National Health Expenditure Data *(2013).*

it is unlikely expenditures will decrease in the foreseeable future.[24] The trend is clearly visible in figure 2. Further, this is an important point to summarize and repeat: Medicaid expansion under the ACA allows a state to pass most of the cost along to taxpayers in other states, but only if it passes some costs along to its own taxpayers as well.

Based on preliminary estimates from CMS, Medicaid expenditures per year are expected to increase by approximately $500 billion between 2012 and 2021—roughly a 108 percent increase.[25] (See figure 3.) It is important to note that CMS assumes universal expansion of the Medicaid program to include the ACA-intended beneficiary group. Even if one argues that it is incorrect to assume universal participation, the issue of increasing Medicaid expenditures has plagued the health insurance program since its inception.

The amount of money spent on Medicaid continues to represent a significant portion of total health care expenditures in the United States. The problems associated with Medicaid expenditures are further evidenced in figures 3 and 4.

Adjusting for inflation, the amount of money spent on Medicaid has significantly increased since the program was first adopted. For FY2013, Medicaid represented roughly 24 percent of state budgets.

Figure 3. Medicaid Expenditures as a Percentage of Total US Health Care Expenditures

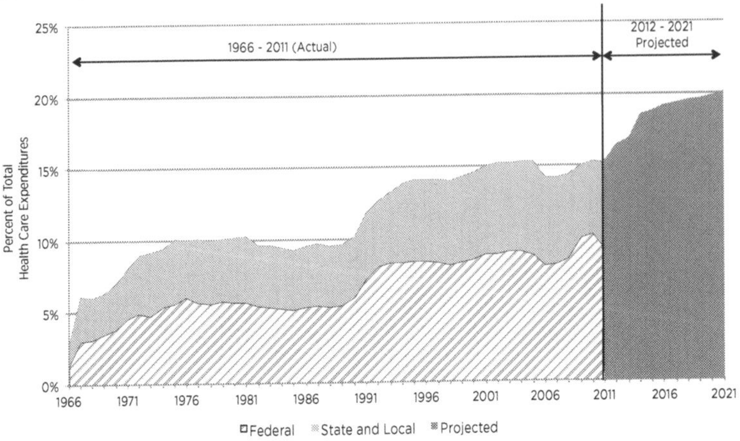

25%
20%
15%
10%
5%
0%
Percent of Total Health Care Expenditures
1966 - 2011 (Actual)
2012 - 2021 Projected
1966
1971
1976
1981
1986
1991
1996
2001
2006
2011
2016
2021
Federal
State and Local
Projected

Source: Centers for Medicare & Medicaid Services, National Health Expenditure Data *(2012).*

Figure 4. Historical Federal and State Medicaid Spending

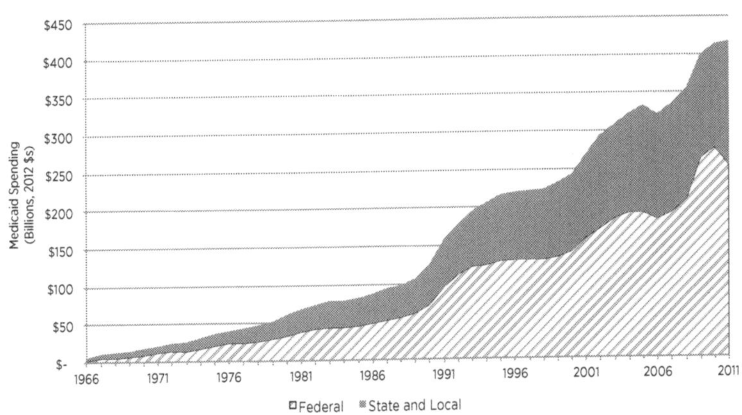

$450
$400
$350
$300
$250
$200
$150
$100
$50
$-
Medicaid Spending (Billions, 2012 $s)
1966
1971
1976
1981
1986
1991
1996
2001
2006
2011
Federal
State and Local

Source: Centers for Medicare & Medicaid Services, National Health Expenditure Data *(2012).*

Some may argue that this increase can be solely attributed to rising health care costs, but research shows that it can be primarily attributed to "changing demographics, increased access and eligibility, service expansions, and waste."[26] Regardless of the cause, Medicaid continues to become a larger share of state budgets. (See figure 5.)

Figure 5. Medicaid Expenditures as a Share of Total State Budgets

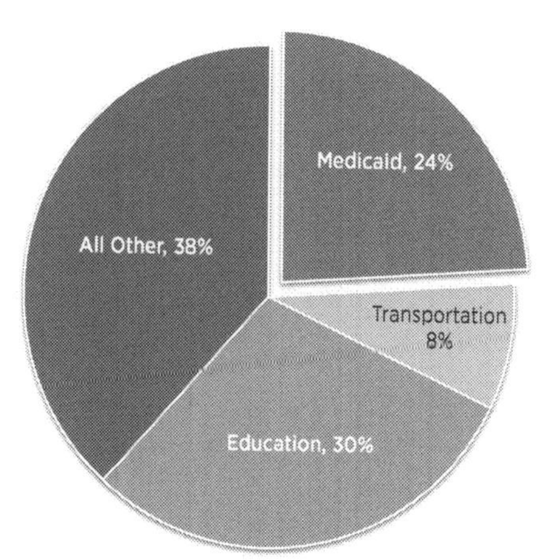

Source: National Association of State Budget Officers, Fiscal Survey of States, 2013.

To reflect the likelihood that not every state in the country will expand Medicaid eligibility, the CBO released a revised report in June 2012 with updated cost estimates. Although the revised estimate suggests that the total Medicaid outlays between 2012 and 2022 will be approximately $289 billion less than originally planned, it projected that federal government exchange subsidies and related spending will increase by $209 billion.[27] This revised estimate warrants further clarification.

To this point, this report has focused solely on the expansion of the Medicaid program. Though no state is required to expand eligibility, every state must have a health insurance exchange ("exchange"). In its simplest form, an exchange is an online marketplace where qualified individuals and small businesses can purchase health insurance. The exchange is supposed to help facilitate the purchase of health insurance by allowing individuals and businesses to compare benefits and prices of different plans. In implementing the exchanges, each state has the option to either establish and operate its own exchange (assuming approval by the HHS secretary), engage in a partnership with the federal government, or opt for a complete federally established and facilitated exchange.[28]

Though numerous stipulations exist, an applicant in the exchange may be eligible for federal subsidies to help pay for an insurance policy offered through the exchange. To be considered for such subsidies, an applicant must not be eligible for "minimum essential coverage" except through the individual health insurance market or an employer-sponsored plan that is either deemed unaffordable or does not provide an ACA-mandated minimum value. The applicant's income must fall between 100 and 400 percent of the FPL.[29] Minimum essential coverage is defined as coverage under the following: (1) a government-sponsored plan; (2) an employer-sponsored plan; (3) plans in the individual market; (4) grandfathered health plans; (5) or any other health benefits coverage recognized by the HHS secretary.[30]

It is important to highlight the threshold established by the ACA because it creates a new incentive for state governments. The ACA effectively created a new beneficiary group characterized by individuals who were previously ineligible for Medicaid and whose income fell below 133 percent of the FPL. For states that opt to expand coverage, Blahous's research suggests coverage will be expanded only for individuals making below 100 percent of the FPL.[31] For a state governor who values maximizing externally financed health benefits while minimizing exposure to the state's budget, this type of expansion would allow citizens to experience higher quality health care at no additional cost to the state.[32]

Unfortunately, this incentive is likely to have a significant impact on the federal government's budget. Assuming that the HHS secretary allows partial expansion, CBO's revised estimates suggest that exchange insurance subsidies and other related spending are expected to cost $1.2 trillion between 2014 and 2024—with costs starting to gradually increase in 2014.[33]

UNCERTAINTY SURROUNDING GROWTH IN HEALTH CARE COSTS

Whether the recent decline in the growth rate of health care costs is a permanent trend or an aberration that will abate is the subject of much current debate (see figure 6). Further, how an aging US population interacts with economic growth, wealth, poverty, retirement security, and the growth rate of health care costs will all directly affect the cost of providing Medicaid coverage. For example, if a higher percentage of an increasingly older society becomes poorer (because of slower economic growth, lack of savings for retirement, etc.) and turns to Medicaid for health coverage, this would in general increase the federal budget outlays for Medicaid. If coupled with a higher-than-estimated growth in medical costs, then the impact on federal spending for Medicaid would be even greater.

President Obama's Council of Economic Advisers released a report near the end of 2013 suggesting that the ACA was responsible for the recent reduction in health care cost growth and will ultimately reduce health care costs.[34] This claim was quickly disputed by several health care experts. For example, in the context of national health expenditures (NHE), Blahous "found that the ACA would increase national health expenditures through 2016."[35] Also, James Capretta, a health care official with the Office of Management and Budget from 2001 to 2004, noted that the slowdown in health care costs did not start with passage of the ACA, but rather, "In 2002, NHE spending per capita rose 8.5 percent and then began to slow over the ensuring years. In 2008, NHE spending per capita rose just 3.7 percent—two years before Obamacare was enacted." Further, Capretta notes that the CMS actuaries estimate the ACA's "Medicaid expansion and new subsidies for insurance offered in the exchanges will greatly increase the demand for health services, and soaring demand always increases prices and costs."[36]

Although the academic debate continues regarding the true causes of the recent slowdown in health care costs, and whether the trend will continue or reverse, it is hard to envision a situation whereby creating a major expansion in the number of people eligible for Medicaid does

Figure 6. Real Per Capita Growth in National Health Expenditures

Data note: Figures for 2012 and 2013 are projections.
Source: Centers for Medicare and Medicaid Services; Census Bureau; Office of Management and Budget.
Produced by Jason Fichtner, Mercatus Center at George Mason University.

not also lead to an increase in the total dollars spent on Medicaid—whether purely because of an increase in the number of people now demanding health care or coupled with an increase in the cost of providing health care. What seems certain, as outlined in this chapter, is that the growth in the federal cost of Medicaid is very likely to continue unabated without significant and meaningful reforms that reduce the number of people covered, reduce the health care services covered, or shift more of the cost onto the private sector and individuals.

CONCLUSION

Given that the ACA is still in its infancy, and regulatory and legislative changes may occur in the near future to address problems with its initial rollout and implementation, it is nonetheless imperative to consider how the ACA will significantly further negatively impact federal budgets and affect the economy at large. To emphasize this point, consider figure 7.

Figure 7. Health Expenditures as a Percentage of Gross Domestic Product

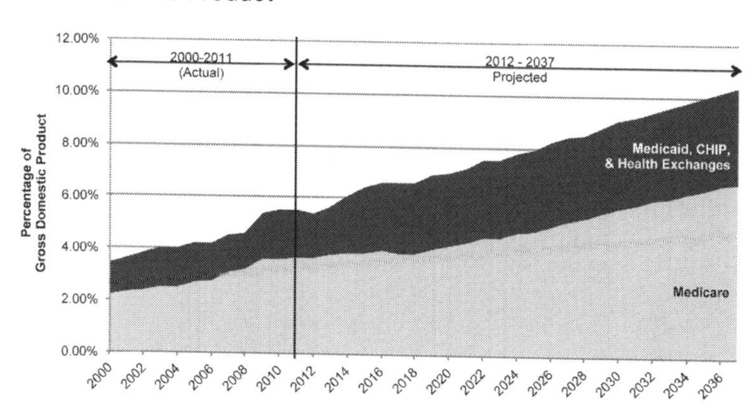

Source: Congressional Budget Office, The 2012 Long-Term Budget Outlook *(2012).*

Examining the data between 2000 and 2036, it is clear that the two largest government health care programs in the country are slowly beginning to represent a larger share of gross domestic product (GDP). With noninterest spending at 22 percent of GDP, it is clear that government health care spending is at unprecedented levels. With or without Medicaid eligibility expansion, Medicaid is on a trajectory to require increasing resources at state and federal levels of government, creating difficult budgetary tradeoffs for both unless major and significant reforms to Medicaid are implemented. These reforms will be covered in the chapters that follow.

NOTES

1. J. K. Iglehart, "The Dilemma of Medicaid," *New England Journal of Medicine* 348, no. 21 (2003): 2140–8; Centers for Medicare & Medicaid Services, *CMS Financial Report, Fiscal Year 2010* (Baltimore, MD: Department of Health & Human Services, 2010), http://www.cms.gov/Research-Statistics-Data-and-Systems/Statistics-Trends-and-Reports/CFOReport/downloads/2010_CMS_Financial_Report.pdf.
2. Centers for Medicare & Medicaid Services, *CMS Financial Report, Fiscal Year 2012* (Baltimore, MD: Department of Health & Human Services, 2012), http://www.cms.gov/Research-Statistics-Data-and-Systems/Statistics-Trends-and-Reports/CFOReport/Downloads/2012_CMS_Financial_Report.pdf.

3. Patient Protection and Affordable Care Act, Pub. L. No. 111-148, 124 Stat. 119 (2010) (codified as amended sections of 42 U.S.C.).
4. See "CBO's Analysis of the Major Health Care Legislation Enacted in March 2010," Before the Subcommittee on Health, Committee on Energy and Commerce, US House of Representatives, 112th Cong. (2011) (statement of Douglas W. Elmendorf, Director of the Congressional Budget Office), http://www.cbo.gov/sites/default/files/cbofiles/ftpdocs/121xx/doc12119/03-30-healthcarelegislation.pdf; and Congressional Budget Office "The Budget and Economic Outlook: 2014 to 2024," February 4, 2014. http://cbo.gov/publication/45010.
5. See Congressional Budget Office, "The Budget and Economic Outlook."
6. See Jennifer Haberkorn, "Medicaid Enrollment Surges Ahead of ACA Sign-Ups," *Politico*, October 29, 2013, http://www.politico.com/story/2013/10/medicaid-enrollment-surges-ahead-of-aca-sign-ups-98977.html.
7. "Eligibility," *Medicaid.gov*, Centers for Medicare & Medicaid Services, accessed November 19, 2013, http://www.medicaid.gov/Medicaid-CHIP-Program-Information/By-Topics/Eligibility/Eligibility.html.
8. "State Medicaid & CHIP Policies for 2014," Medicaid.gov, Centers for Medicare & Medicaid Services, accessed November 19, 2013, http://www.medicaid.gov/Medicaid-CHIP-Program-Information/By-State/By-State.html.
9. "Eligibility," *Medicaid.gov*.
10. 78 Fed. Reg. 5182–3 (January 24, 2013).
11. Martha Heberlein et al., "Getting into Gear for 2014: Findings from a 50-State Survey of Eligibility, Enrollment, Renewal, and Cost-Sharing Policies in Medicaid and CHIP, 2012–2013" (Washington, DC: Kaiser Commission on Medicaid and the Uninsured, Henry J. Kaiser Family Foundation, January 2013), http://kff.org/medicaid/report/getting-into-gear-for-2014-findings-from-a-50-state-survey-of-eligibility-enrollment-renewal-and-cost-sharing-policies-in-medicaid-and-chip-2012-2013/.
12. Gretchen Engquist and Peter Burns, "Health Insurance Flexibility and Accountability Initiative: Opportunities and Issues for the States," *State Coverage Initiatives* 3, no. 2 (2002): 1–6.
13. Ibid.
14. "Waivers," *Medicaid.gov*, Centers for Medicare & Medicaid Services, accessed November 19, 2013, http://www.medicaid.gov/Medicaid-CHIP-Program-Information/By-Topics/Waivers/Waivers.html.
15. Kathryn Linehan, "The Basics: Medicaid Financing" (Washington, DC: National Health Policy Forum, George Washington University, February 13, 2013), http://www.nhpf.org/library/the-basics/Basics_MedicaidFinancing_02-13-13.pdf.
16. Ibid.
17. National Conference of State Legislatures, "The Affordable Care Act: A Brief Summary" (March 2011); Centers for Medicare & Medicaid Services, *CMS Financial Report, Fiscal Year 2011* (Baltimore, MD: Department of Health & Human Services, 2011), http://www.cms.gov/Research-Statistics-Data-and-Systems/Statistics-Trends-and-Reports/CFOReport/downloads/2011_CMS_Financial_Report.pdf.
18. Ibid.
19. MaryBeth Musumeci, "A Guide to the Supreme Court's Affordable Care Act Decision"

(publication #8332, Henry J. Kaiser Family Foundation, Menlo Park, CA, July 2012), http://kff.org/health-reform/issue-brief/a-guide-to-the-supreme-courts-affordable/.

20. National Federation of Independent Business v. Sebelius, 567 U.S. ____, 51 (2012).

21. Ibid.

22. Linehan, "The Basics."

23. Charles Blahous, "The Affordable Care Act's Optional Medicaid Expansion: Considerations Facing State Governments" (Mercatus Research, Mercatus Center at George Mason University, Arlington, VA, March 5, 2013), 20, http://mercatus.org/publication/affordable-care-acts-optional-medicaid-expansion-considerations-facing-state-governments.

24. National Association of State Budget Officers, *The Fiscal Survey of States, 2012* (2012); US Department of Commerce, *Statistical Abstract of the United States*, 90th ed. (1969).

25. Centers for Medicare and Medicaid Services, *CMS Financial Report, Fiscal Year 2013* (Baltimore, MD: Department of Health & Human Services, 2013), http://www.cms.gov/Research-Statistics-Data-and-Systems/Statistics-Trends-and-Reports/CFOReport/Downloads/2013_CMS_Financial_Report.pdf.

26. Scott Beaulier and Brandon Pizzola, "The Political Economy of Medicaid: Evidence from Five Reforming States" (Mercatus on Policy, Mercatus Center at George Mason University, Arlington, VA, April 2012).

27. Congressional Budget Office, "Estimates for the Insurance Coverage Provisions of the Affordable Care Act Updated for the Recent Supreme Court Decision" (2012).

28. Bernadette Fernandez and Annie L. Mach, "Health Insurance Exchanges under the Patient Protection and Affordable Care Act (ACA)," R42663 (Washington, DC: Congressional Research Service, 2013).

29. Ibid.

30. Annie L. Mach, M. Scales, and J. Mulvey, "Individual Mandate and Related Information Requirements under ACA," R41331 (Washington, DC: Congressional Research Service, July 22, 2013).

31. Blahous, "The Affordable Care Act's Optional Medicaid Expansion."

32. Ibid.

33. Congressional Budget Office, "Estimates for the Insurance Coverage Provisions of the Affordable Care Act Updated for the Recent Supreme Court Decision," and "The Budget and Economic Outlook: 2014 to 2024."

34. Executive Office of the President, Council of Economic Advisers, *Trends in Health Care Cost Growth and the Role of the Affordable Care Act* (November 2013).

35. Charles Blahous, "No Grounds for Claim That Obamacare Lowers Healthcare Costs," November 25, 2013, e21, http://www.economics21.org/commentary/no-grounds-claim-obamacare-lowers-healthcare-costs.

36. James Capretta, "Another Broken Promise: Obamacare Is Driving Costs Up, Not Down," *Weekly Standard*, November 26, 2013, http://www.aei.org/article/health/healthcare-reform/ppaca/another-broken-promise-obamacare-is-driving-costs-up-not-down/.

CHAPTER 4:
THE STATE SIDE OF THE BUDGET EQUATION

NINA OWCHARENKO

Medicaid consumes a significant portion of state budgets. Taking into account significant federal contributions, Medicaid is the single largest budget item in most state budgets, surpassing elementary and secondary education. In 2012, 24 percent of state budgets went to Medicaid. Medicaid spending is expected to climb in the future due to increased enrollment, including Medicaid expansion in the Patient Protection and Affordable Care Act (ACA),[1] and increased costs of providing medical services in general.

To control spending, states typically use a variety of techniques, including adjusting reimbursement rates for providers, restricting eligibility and enrollment, limiting benefits and services, and adopting care management tools, such as managed care. Some states have also recommended more structural financing changes, such as block grants, as a means to better control costs over the long term. However, just as states are looking to control costs, many are also pursuing eligibility and benefit expansions. (See chapter 1, page 9, for an explanation of the incentives that states face to maximize their federal Medicaid funds while controlling their own costs.)

The current federal–state funding structure creates conflicting incentives that perpetuate these fiscal challenges. Efforts to influence the financing at the federal and state level will likely continue without reform.

HOW IS THE PROGRAM FUNDED?

The federal government pays a share of Medicaid costs and the states are responsible for the remaining share. The federal share is calculated by the federal medical assistance percentage (FMAP) formula and adjusted annually. In general, this percentage is determined based on each state's personal income versus the national average income.[2]

States also receive enhanced federal funds for serving specific populations, such as Native Americans and Alaskans. They also receive enhanced federal funding for providing certain services, such as family planning, and for opting to extend eligibility or services to nonmandatory groups.[3] And administrative costs, which account for about 5 percent of Medicaid spending, are funded separately and typically matched at a 50 percent rate by the federal government, but with exceptions as well.[4]

In response to the economic downturn, the American Recovery and Reinvestment Act of 2009 provided a temporary increase in the federal match rate to states from October 2008 to June 2011. The average federal share of Medicaid spending in 2010 increased to a high of 67 percent, leaving the average state share at a low of 33 percent.[5] In 2012, when the additional federal funds expired, the average federal share dropped back to its historic average of 57 percent, increasing the average state share to 43 percent.

Most recently, the ACA provides an enhanced federal match to cover costs for expanding coverage to childless adults earning up to 138 percent of the federal poverty level. States will receive a 100 percent federal match rate for this expansion group in 2014, 2015, and 2016, and then the federal share will gradually phase down to 90 percent by 2020. However, this enhanced match is only for the newly eligible population. States will continue to receive the standard federal matching rates for currently eligible populations, including those previously eligible but not enrolled. By 2020, combining both enhanced and standard rates, the average federal share of Medicaid spending is projected to be 60 percent, leaving states with 40 percent on average.[6]

The ACA also increased the federal matching rate for primary care providers in Medicaid by raising payment rates for this group of physicians to Medicare-level rates. This enhanced federal match is temporary and is scheduled to expire at the end of 2014.[7]

Counterintuitively, total Medicaid spending is typically highest in wealthier states, with a 50 percent match. As American Enterprise Institute scholar Robert Helms points out, "Even though wealthier states have lower matching rates, they have expanded their programs to a greater extent than the states that typically have higher proportions of poor people."[8]

WHAT PERCENTAGE OF STATE BUDGETS GO TOWARD MEDICAID?

In terms of total state expenditures, Medicaid represents the single largest item in state budgets. Medicaid represented 22.2 percent of spending across all states in FY2010, 23.7 in FY2011, and an estimated 23.9 percent in FY2012.[9] To compare, spending for elementary and secondary education was 20.4 percent in FY2010, 20.2 percent in FY2011, and estimated 19.8 percent in FY2012.[10]

It is worth noting, however, that these total state expenditures take into account federal contributions. Federal grants to Medicaid represented 62.7 percent of total state Medicaid spending in FY2011, while state general fund spending represented 26.9 percent.[11] By comparison, federal grants represented only 21.0 percent of total elementary and secondary education expenditures in FY2011, while state general fund expenditures represented 66.5 percent.[12] (See figure 1.)

Figure 1. Total State Expenditures for Elementary and Secondary Education (*left*) and Medicaid (*right*) by Funding Source, Fiscal Year 2011

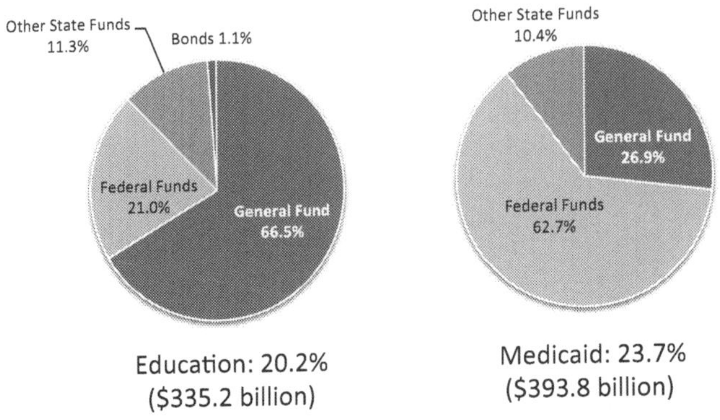

Source: National Association of State Budget Officers, "State Expenditure Report: Examining Fiscal 2010-2012 State Spending."

STATE SPENDING BY ENROLLEE, GROUP, AND SERVICE

State Medicaid spending varies by state for many reasons, including eligibility, benefits, and cost of care. States are required to provide care to certain mandatory populations and for certain mandatory services.[13] But, beyond these designations, states are permitted to extend their Medicaid programs to serve certain optional populations and provide certain optional services. Furthermore, states have the latitude to administer their programs differently in other ways, such as determining provider reimbursement levels. Because of such variations, no two Medicaid programs are alike at the state level.

According to the Henry J. Kaiser Family Foundation, national per enrollee spending in FY2009 was $5,527.[14] The highest per enrollee spending by state was $9,577 in Connecticut, $9,143 in the District of Columbia, and $8,960 in New York. The lowest per enrollee spending by state was $3,527 in California, $3,979 in Georgia, and $4,081 in Alabama.

By group, 65 percent of national Medicaid spending in FY2009 went to the elderly and disabled, while the remaining 35 percent was spent on adults and children.[15] State-level spending on the elderly and disabled ranged from a high of 77 percent in the District of Columbia to 76 percent in North Dakota and New Jersey, and a low of 51 percent in Delaware, 54 percent in Alaska, and 55 percent in Georgia. State level spending on working-aged adults and children ranged from a high of 59 percent in Arizona and New Mexico and 49 percent in Delaware, and a low of 24 percent in New Jersey and North Dakota and 27 percent in West Virginia and Pennsylvania.

By services, 65.6 percent of national Medicaid spending in FY2011 was on acute care services and 30.2 percent on long-term care services.[16] State-level spending on acute care ranged from a high of 91.9 percent in Hawaii, 88.9 percent in New Mexico, and 88.3 percent in Vermont, to a low of 37.6 percent in North Dakota, 45.4 percent in New Hampshire, and 50 percent in Connecticut. State-level spending on long-term care ranged from a high of 62.1 percent in North Dakota and 46.7 percent in Connecticut and Wyoming, to a low of 6.9 percent in Hawaii, 8.9 percent in Vermont, and 10.3 percent in New Mexico.

WHAT ARE THE STATE MEDICAID SPENDING TRAJECTORIES?

While year-to-year spending fluctuates, the long-term spending trend in Medicaid remains on an upward trajectory. In 1990, combined federal and state spending on Medicaid was $72.2 billion, with the state share at $31.3 billion and a total enrollment of 22.9 million.[17] By 2000, total Medicaid spending increased to $206.2 billion, with the state share at $89.2 billion and enrollment at 34.5 million. In 2010, total Medicaid spending reached $401.5 billion, with the state share at $131.7 billion and total enrollment estimated to be 53.7 million. (See figure 2.)

The Government Accountability Office's (GAO's) state and local fiscal outlook report warns of the following: "The primary driver of fiscal challenges for the state and local government sector in the long term continues to be the projected growth in health-related costs.

Figure 2. Total Medicaid Spending and State Medicaid Spending, Historical and Projected

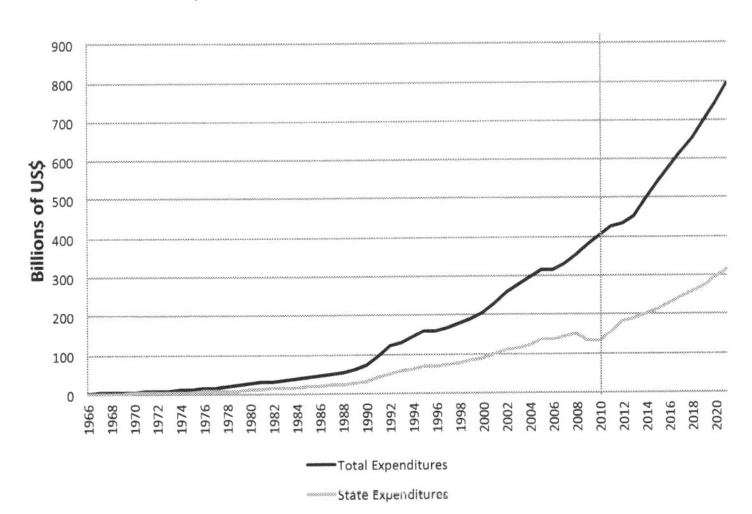

Source: Centers for Medicare and Medicaid Services, 2012 Actuarial Report on the Financial Outlook for Medicaid.

Specifically, state and local expenditures on Medicaid and the cost of health care compensation for state and local government employees and retirees are projected to grow more than GDP."[18] In FY2011, Medicaid spending represented 2.8 percent of GDP and is expected to reach 3.2 percent of GDP by FY2021.[19]

In its 2008 report, before the enactment of the ACA, the Centers for Medicare and Medicaid Services, Office of the Actuary projected that combined federal and state spending on Medicaid would reach $673.7 billion in FY2017, with the state share at $290.3 billion and total enrollment reaching 55.1 million.[20] After enactment of the ACA, the Actuary's 2011 report projected that total Medicaid spending would reach $871.1 billion in 2020, with the state share reaching $340.0 billion and enrollment topping 85 million.[21]

But predicting future spending is always tentative and the Supreme Court decision in *National Federation of Independent Business v. Sebelius*, which overturned a key ACA Medicaid provision, underscores that uncertainty. The Supreme Court decision clarified that states that chose not to expand their Medicaid program to childless adults would lose only the enhanced funding for the expansion population—not all federal funding for Medicaid.[22]

The 2012 Centers for Medicare and Medicaid Services, Office of the Actuary report adjusted its projections based on the Supreme Court decision and now estimates that Medicaid expenditures will increase at an average annual rate of 6.4 percent. By 2020, total spending is now projected to be $746.2 billion, with the state share of these expenditures expected to be $296.8 billion and enrollment at 77.4 million.[23]

TRENDING UPWARD: HIGHER ENROLLMENT AND HIGHER MEDICAL COSTS

The projected spending increases in Medicaid are a result of both rising enrollment and increasing medical costs. Even before millions of childless adults are added to the program, existing demographic challenges are substantial in Medicaid. For example, Medicare beneficiaries also enrolled in Medicaid made up 15 percent of enrollment while consuming 38 percent of Medicaid spending in 2009.[24]

According to GAO, "The increase in the number of people 85 or older in the next 10 years is expected to have a major effect on long-term care spending for Medicaid. As such, a key driver of federal spending for both Medicare and Medicaid is the aging population. Enrollment from this population did not change as a result of the PPACA."[25]

The Actuary's report estimates enrollment is expected to jump from 55.7 million in FY2011 to 77.9 million in 2021. Enrollment of the low-income elderly is projected to reach 6.5 million and that of the disabled to reach 10.2 million. Enrollment of children is projected to reach 31.7 million, while enrollment of previously eligible adults is expected to reach 15.9 million. In addition, 12.6 million of newly eligible adults are projected to enroll.[26] The Actuary's report also points out the following: "Although much of Medicaid's expenditure growth (past and future) is due to expansion of eligibility criteria, the 'per

Figure 3. 2011 and 2021 Per Enrollee Expenditures, by Category

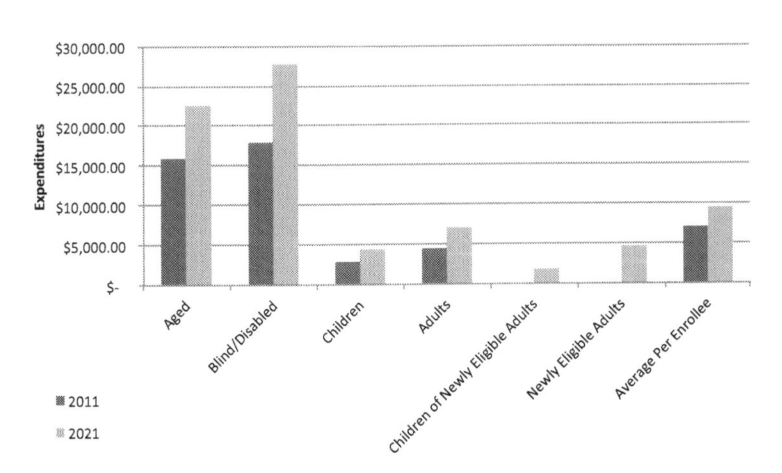

Source: Centers for Medicare and Medicaid Services, 2012 Actuarial Report on the Financial Outlook for Medicaid.

enrollee' costs for Medicaid have also usually increased significantly faster than per capita GDP."[27]

According to the projections, total Medicaid spending per beneficiary will also rise to an average of $9,532 by FY2021, compared with $6,982 in FY2011.[28] Average spending per disabled person will rise to $27,647 by FY2021; average spending per elderly individual will rise to $22,446; average spending per child will rise to $4,389; average spending on previously eligible adults will rise to $ 6,939; and spending will average $4,684 for newly eligible adults. (See figure 3.)

STATE EFFORTS TO CONTROL MEDICAID COSTS AND SPENDING

Faced with higher spending, states—as administrators of this joint federal–state program—play a significant role in determining Medicaid costs and spending. Most recently, the Actuary's report points out the following: "Following the expiration of temporary increases in the Federal matching rate, the States' share of Medicaid expenditures have grown rapidly over the last 2 years—nearly 40 percent—and the States have acted to reduce provider payment rates and/or optional benefits. Their actions had a substantial impact in 2012 and emphasize the difficulty in balancing Medicaid against other government programs in the context of States' budgets."[29]

States focus their efforts to control costs through a variety of policy initiatives. The Henry J. Kaiser Family Foundation's 50 State Annual Medicaid Budget Survey offers an overview of such state budget actions. It found that 43 states implemented at least one cost containment measure in FY2013 and the same number plan to do so in FY2014.[30] At the same time, 46 states reported implementing a program improvement in FY2013 and 47 states expect to in FY2014.

Provider rates. One of the most common tools used by states to control Medicaid costs is to adjust payment rates for health care providers serving Medicaid patients. Thirty-nine states implemented some rate restrictions on providers in FY2013, and 34 states adopted restrictions for FY2014.[31] Hospitals and nursing homes were most targeted.

Of course, one consequence of provider cuts is that fewer providers will participate in the program. Today, physicians are less willing to accept new Medicaid patients.[32] The access issue will be increasingly important as millions of new patients are expected to join the program as a result of the ACA. Possibly because of these challenges, the Kaiser survey found that 40 states increased certain provider rates in FY2013 and 44 adopted increases for FY2014.[33] As noted earlier, the ACA does provide additional federal dollars to states to increase payment rates for primary care physicians in order to meet Medicare levels. This boost in federal funding, however, is temporary, and it remains unclear whether states will resume lower reimbursement rates once these federal funds expire at the end of 2014.

Eligibility and enrollment. States have also considered limiting eligibility and enrollment to control Medicaid growth. Policies such as scaling back eligible populations to lower income levels and freezing or capping enrollment for some groups have been initiated by some states. However, such changes have been more limited than in previous years. According to the Annual Medicaid Budget Survey, 5 states scaled back eligibility for adults in FY2013,[34] whereas in FY2006, for example, 18 states adopted eligibility restrictions.[35]

Some of this change is likely a result of the "maintenance of effort" (MOE) requirement in the American Recovery and Reinvestment Act of 2009, which prohibited states from implementing policy changes that would restrict eligibility or enrollment, as a condition of receiving the additional federal funding.[36] Some is a likely result of the overall push of the ACA to expand, not restrict, eligibility and enrollment. In fact, the Kaiser survey found 45 states reported adopting enrollment expansions or enhancements (such as streamlining application and renewal processes) for FY2014.[37]

Benefits. Adjusting benefits and benefit designs are other cost control tools used by the states. These changes can focus on eliminating or limiting a type of benefit or service. For example, in FY2013, 14 states adopted some level of benefit restrictions.[38] Of those, 5 states reported eliminating at least one benefit all together.[39]

Pharmaceutical benefits are another area that states target for cost control. According to the Henry J. Kaiser Family Foundation survey, 24 states issued some cost containment measures to manage pharmaceutical costs for FY2013 and 25 adopted new policies for FY2014.[40] Policies range from preferred drug lists, to supplemental rebates, to limiting the number of allowable prescriptions.

States also use premiums and cost sharing to manage costs. The Deficit Reduction Act of 2005 provided additional leeway for states to require enrollees at various income levels to participate in cost-sharing arrangements, whether premiums or copays. In FY2013, 39 states reported premium requirements for some group in Medicaid.[41]

Care management. States are looking to control costs by more effectively coordinating and managing care delivery for Medicaid enrollees. Most notable is the shift toward Medicaid managed care. States are able to control costs by capping reimbursement to private insurers. According to the Medicaid and CHIP Payment and Access

Commission: "In 1995, 15 percent of Medicaid enrollees were enrolled in such an arrangement. By 2011, half of all Medicaid enrollees were enrolled in a comprehensive risk-based plan."[42]

States are also looking to adopt policies focused on the most costly enrollees—the disabled and the elderly. Only 24 percent of enrollees are elderly or disabled, but they represent 64 percent of total Medicaid spending. According to the Congressional Research Service, long-term care services account for more than one-third of all Medicaid spending.[43] Increasingly, states are focused on adopting policies to better coordinate care and costs for these long-term care services.

Other cost containment efforts. In the past, some states' cost containment strategies looked beyond their existing scope of authority and turned to federal waivers[44] to experiment with larger budget strategies. Vermont and Rhode Island are two notable examples.[45] Both states negotiated an agreement with the federal government to accept capped federal funding over a period of time with some policy changes. The concept behind these initiatives was to demonstrate that states could keep spending below the federal cap if given additional tools to manage the program.

Along these same lines, there is growing interest in the states to advance block grant concepts for Medicaid. The Republican Governors Association sent a letter in support of the FY2012 House budget proposal that included a Medicaid block grant structure.[46] (See chapter 7, page 138, for more information on the mechanics of block grants.)

It could be argued that not opting for the ACA Medicaid expansion is also a form of cost containment. Analysis shows the long-term cost implications of the Medicaid expansion may outweigh any temporary, short-term benefit.[47]

WHAT INCENTIVES DO STATES FACE GIVEN FEDERAL FUNDING FORMULAS?

The open-ended nature of the Medicaid funding structure and the joint federal–state partnership creates perverse incentives at both the state and federal levels. States are driven to leverage as many federal dollars as possible, and the federal government uses its funding power to persuade states to adopt certain policies. For every dollar a state puts in, the federal government matches one for one and sometimes provides even more.[48]

As noted, the federal grants are a key component of the state budgets. Unfortunately, this leads states to spend funds on Medicaid they otherwise would not have. The ACA is a good example. Total Medicaid spending is expected to increase by 13 percent in FY2014 for states opting for the new ACA Medicaid expansion (and its enhanced federal funding), compared with 6.8 percent in states opting not to expand.[49] Thus, states opting for the expansion are fueling overall Medicaid spending.

The incentive to maximize and leverage unlimited federal dollars has led states to develop financing schemes such as provider taxes, where states tax Medicaid providers in order to gain the federal match and then "repay" these providers with Medicaid reimbursement.[50] Although these provider tax techniques are under greater scrutiny, states' use of them continues to grow. According to the Kaiser survey: "At the beginning of FY 2003, a total of 32 states had at least one provider tax in place. ... By FY 2013, all but one state (Alaska) has one or more provider taxes in place."[51]

Federal Medicaid funding policies also create perverse incentives for the states to adopt certain federal policies, such as expanding coverage, services, and benefits. This is most evident in the use of the enhanced match rate under the ACA to entice states to extend Medicaid eligibility to the childless adult population.[52] Another example is CHIP, which uses enhanced federal Medicaid match rates to coerce states into agreeing to expand coverage to children above the normal Medicaid eligibility levels. Other examples include enhanced federal match rates for family planning services, certain long-term care initiatives, and for the adoption of health information technologies.[53]

CONCLUSION

The fiscal challenges facing Medicaid are real. As the GAO report on the state and local fiscal outlook found: "The state and local government sector continues to face near-term and long-term fiscal challenges which add to the nation's overall fiscal challenges."[54] Such warnings suggest that policy changes at the federal and state levels will be needed to address the long-term viability of the program. In the meantime, it is likely that the pressure to control Medicaid spending will continue to fall on the states, which in turn will push states to continue to explore new ways to address the fiscal challenges in Medicaid.

NOTES

1. Patient Protection and Affordable Care Act, Pub. L. No. 111-148, 124 Stat. 119 (2010) (codified as amended sections of 42 U.S.C.).
2. See Joseph Antos's more detailed explanation in chapter 1.
3. Henry J. Kaiser Family Foundation, "Medicaid Financing: An Overview of the Federal Medicaid Match Rate," September 2012, 7, http://www.kaiserfamilyfoundation.files.wordpress.com/2013/01/8352.pdf.
4. Ibid., 9.
5. Office of the Actuary, Centers for Medicare and Medicaid Services, US Department of Health and Human Services, "2012 Actuarial Report on the Financial Outlook for Medicaid," March 2013, 22, http://www.medicaid.gov/Medicaid-CHIP-Program-Information/By-Topics/Financing-and-Reimbursement/Downloads/medicaid-actuarial-report-2012.pdf.
6. Office of the Actuary, "2012 Actuarial Report on the Financial Outlook for Medicaid," 22.
7. Health Care and Education Reconciliation Act of 2010, Pub. L. No. 111–152, § 1202 (enacted March 30, 2010). This law made several changes to the underlying Patient Protection and Affordable Care Act of 2010, Pub. L. No. 111-148 (enacted March 23, 2010).
8. Robert Helms, "Medicaid: The Forgotten Issue in Health Reform," American Enterprise Institute Outlook No. 14, November 2009, 2, http://www.aei.org/files/2009/11/06/14-HPO-Helms-g.pdf.
9. National Association of State Budget Officers, "State Expenditure Report," 2012, 9, http://www.nasbo.org/sites/default/files/State%20Expenditure%20Report_1.pdf.
10. Ibid.
11. Ibid., 45.
12. Ibid., 14.
13. For a discussion of the mandatory and optional populations and services, see Henry J.

Kaiser Family Foundation, "Medicaid: An Overview of Spending on 'Mandatory' vs. 'Optional' Populations and Services," June 2005, http://kaiserfamilyfoundation.files .wordpress.com/2013/01/medicaid-an-overview-of-spending-on.pdf.

14. Henry J. Kaiser Family Foundation, "Medicaid: A Primer," March 2013, 43, http://kaiserfamilyfoundation.files.wordpress.com/2010/06/7334-05.pdf.
15. Ibid., 42.
16. Ibid., 44.
17. Office of the Actuary, "2012 Actuarial Report," 22.
18. US General Accountability Office, "State and Local Governments' Fiscal Outlook," April 2013, 5, http://www.gao.gov/assets/660/654255.pdf.
19. Office of the Actuary, "2012 Actuarial Report," 49, 50.
20. Office of the Actuary, Centers for Medicare and Medicaid Services, US Department of Health and Human Services, "2008 Actuarial Report on the Financial Outlook for Medicaid," October 2008, 16, 18, http://medicaid.gov/Medicaid-CHIP-Program -Information/By-Topics/Financing-and-Reimbursement/Downloads/medicaid -actuarial-report-2008.pdf.
21. Office of the Actuary, Centers for Medicare and Medicaid Services, US Department of Health and Human Services, "2011 Actuarial Report on the Financial Outlook for Medicaid," March 16, 2012, 19, http://medicaid.gov/Medicaid-CHIP-Program -Information/By-Topics/Financing-and-Reimbursement/Downloads/medicaid -actuarial-report-2011.pdf.
22. For a discussion of the new options, see Charles Blahous, "The Affordable Care Act's Optional Medicaid Expansion: Considerations Facing State Governments," Mercatus Center at George Mason University, March 5, 2013, http://mercatus.org/sites/default /files/Blahous_MedicaidExpansion_v1.pdf.
23. Office of the Actuary, "2012 Actuarial Report," 22.
24. Kaiser Family Foundation, "Medicaid: A Primer," 10.
25. US Government Accountability Office, "Patient Protection and Affordable Care Act: Effect on Long-Term Federal Budget Outlook Largely Depends on Whether Cost Containment Sustained," January 2013, 24, http://www.gao.gov/assets/660/651702.pdf.
26. Office of the Actuary, "2012 Actuarial Report," figure 4, 28.
27. Ibid., i.
28. Ibid., figure 5, 30.
29. Ibid., i.
30. Vernon Smith et al., "Medicaid in a Historic Time of Transition: Results from a 50-State Medicaid Budget Survey for State Fiscal Years 2013 and 2014," Henry J. Kaiser Family Foundation, October 7, 2013, 86, 87, http://kaiserfamilyfoundation.files.wordpress.com /2013/10/8498-medicaid-in-a-historic-time4.pdf.
31. Ibid., 47.
32. Sandra L. Decker, "In 2011 Nearly One-Third of Physicians Said They Would Not Accept New Medicaid Patients, But Rising Fees May Help," *Health Affairs* 31, no. 8 (2012): 1673–79.
33. Ibid.

34. Smith et al., "Medicaid in a Historic Time of Transition," 25.

35. Vernon Smith et al., "Low Medicaid Spending Growth amid Rebounding State Revenues: Results from a 50-State Medicaid Budget Survey State Fiscal Years 2006 and 2007" (Henry J. Kaiser Family Foundation, October 2006), 25, http://kaiserfamilyfoundation.files.wordpress.com/2013/01/7569.pdf.

36. The Affordable Care Act extended these restrictions until 2014 for adults and 2019 for children.

37. Smith et al., "Medicaid in a Historic Time of Transformation," 4.

38. Ibid., 54.

39. Ibid.

40. Ibid., 55.

41. Ibid., 51.

42. Medicaid and CHIP Payment and Access Commission, "Medicaid Managed Care," *MACFacts*, April 2013, https://sites.google.com/a/macpac.gov/macpac/publications /MACFacts-ManagedCare_2013-04.pdf?attredirects=1.

43. Kirsten J. Colello, "Medicaid Coverage of Long-Term Services and Supports," Congressional Research Service, December 5, 2013, 1, http://www.fas.org/sgp/crs/misc /R43328.pdf.

44. See James Capretta, chapter 7 in this publication, "Reforming Medicaid."

45. Robert Wood Johnson Foundation, "Rhode Island Pursues Health Reforms in Public and Private Sectors," State Coverage Initiatives, February 18, 2009, http://www .statecoverage.org/node/1343.

46. Sarah Kliff and J. Lester Feder, "GOP Governors Want Medicaid Block Grants," *Politico*, February 28, 2011, http://www.politico.com/news/stories/0211/50288.html.

47. Blahous, "The Affordable Care Act's Optional Medicaid Expansion."

48. For a discussion on the FMAP Multiplier, see Henry J. Kaiser Family Foundation, "Medicaid Financing: An Overview of the Federal Medicaid Match Rate," 4.

49. Smith et al., "Medicaid in a Historic Time of Transition," 19.

50. Ralph Lindeman, "Medicaid Faces Possible Funding Cuts, Health Law Implementation Challenges," *Daily Report for Executives*, Bureau of National Affairs, January 16, 2013.

51. Smith et al., "Medicaid in a Historic Time of Transition," 50.

52. Carter C. Price and Christine Eibner, "For States That Opt out of Medicaid Expansion: 3.6 Million Fewer Insured and $8.4 Billion Less in Federal Payments," *Health Affairs* 32, no. 6 (2013): 1030–36. For an opposing view, see Edmund Haislmaier and Drew Gonshorowski, "State Lawmaker's Guide to Evaluating Medicaid Expansion Projections," *Issue Brief* No. 3720 (Heritage Foundation, September 7, 2012), http://www .heritage.org/research/reports/2012/09/state-lawmakers-guide-to-evaluating-medicaid -expansion-projections.

53. Henry J. Kaiser Family Foundation, "Medicaid Financing."

54. US General Accountability Office, "State and Local Governments' Fiscal Outlook," 1.

PART 3:

THE AFFORDABLE CARE ACT AND MEDICAID

CHAPTER 5: MEDICAID UNDER THE AFFORDABLE CARE ACT

CHARLES P. BLAHOUS

The 2010 passage of the Patient Protection and Affordable Care Act (PPACA), more commonly referred to as the Affordable Care Act (ACA),[1] vastly increased projected Medicaid costs. One of the core objectives of the ACA was to expand considerably the ranks of Americans with health insurance coverage, with Medicaid serving as the primary vehicle for covering the previously uninsured poor. The ACA's expansion of Medicaid coverage will cause Medicaid costs to increase significantly, with these increases concentrated on the federal share of total Medicaid expenditures.

The ACA dramatically expanded the numbers of those eligible for Medicaid coverage by mandating that participating states offer coverage to all childless adults with incomes below 133 percent of the federal poverty level (FPL). The income eligibility threshold was effectively set at 138 percent of FPL by another statutory provision that established a 5 percent income exclusion.[2]

The federal government attempted to cushion the financial blow that this dramatic coverage expansion would embody for the states by financing with federal funds 100 percent of Medicaid costs for the newly eligible population in the first three years of 2014–16, a percentage that will gradually decline to 90 percent by the year 2020.

Medicaid is a joint federal–state program in which state participation is technically voluntarily; the federal government cannot constitutionally force states to participate, though all states do. But at the same time, the federal government—through the auspices of the secretary of Health and Human Services (HHS)—has the statutory power to deny federal Medicaid funding to a state if the secretary determines that it is not in compliance with federal Medicaid law's benefit and eligibility requirements.[3] With the ACA having expanded Medicaid's mandatory coverage standards, the federal government essentially gave itself the power to deny Medicaid funding to any state that did not fully participate in the expansion. The only alternative to full expansion left to the states per the language of the ACA was the politically implausible one of ending their participation in Medicaid altogether.

This dynamic was changed significantly by the US Supreme Court's June 2012 ruling on the constitutionality of the ACA. The court upheld most of the ACA's provisions, most notably its requirement that individuals carry health insurance or be subject to a new federal tax.[4] But in the same ruling, the court struck down the federal government's ability to enforce its mandated Medicaid expansion by withholding existing Medicaid funds from states that declined to comply. By eliminating the federal government's power to enforce it, the court's action effectively made the ACA's Medicaid expansion optional for the states.

The court's decision changed estimates of the projected cost of the ACA, and in particular of its Medicaid expansion provisions. Prior to the decision, it was generally assumed that all states would participate in the expansion. Afterward, because of the conflicting incentives facing states in the wake of the court ruling as well as policy decisions announced by many state governments around the nation, it became clear that some states would not participate in the Medicaid expansion.[5] But until all states have announced and implemented their decisions, Medicaid expansion participation levels can only be very roughly estimated. The Congressional Budget Office's (CBO's) latest

Figure 1. Projected Federal Medicaid Costs, With and Without ACA Medicaid Expansion

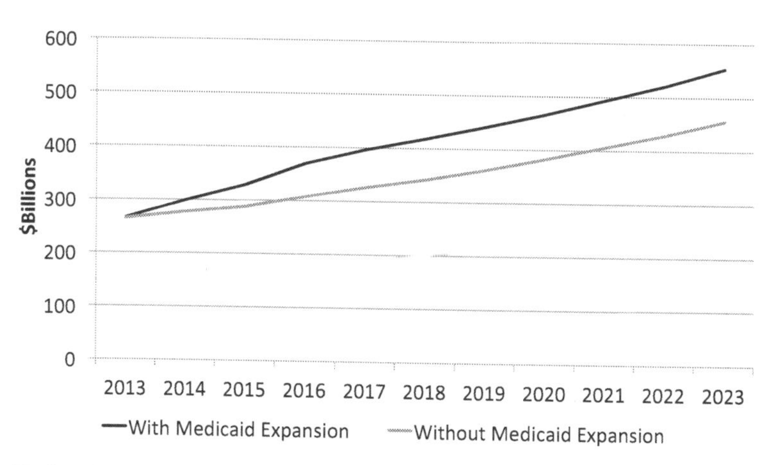

Note: Cost projections are based on CBO assumptions regarding state participation.
Sources: Congressional Budget Office, "CBO's May 2013 Estimate of the Effects of the Affordable Care Act on Health Insurance Coverage," table 2, May 2013; Congressional Budget Office, "Medicaid Spending and Enrollment Detail for CBO's May 2013 Baseline," May 2013.

estimates are that two-thirds of potentially newly eligible individuals reside in states that will voluntarily participate in the ACA expansion, resulting in a total Medicaid coverage increase of 13 million by 2021, on top of a baseline estimate of 34 million projected in the absence of the ACA.[6] This expansion would in turn add $87 billion annually to federal Medicaid and Children's Health Insurance Program (CHIP) outlays by 2021, bringing total federal Medicaid expenditures in that year to $493 billion.[7]

In effect, CBO anticipates that the ACA's Medicaid expansion, even if only partially implemented by the states, will add more than 21 percent to annual federal Medicaid costs by 2021. These cost increases will be added to federal Medicaid costs that were already projected to rise substantially even before the ACA's Medicaid expansion was enacted, as shown in figure 1.

CBO's projections are similar to those made by other federal estimators, including the Chief Actuary of the Centers for Medicare and

Medicaid Services (CMS). In its 2012 actuarial report, the Office of the Chief Actuary estimated that federal Medicaid costs will reach $478 billion annually by 2021.[8] This is based on an assumption that in 2014, 55 percent of the potentially newly Medicaid-eligible population will reside in states that choose to expand, a percentage rising to 65 percent in 2015 and thereafter. This participation assumption is just slightly lower than the two-thirds assumption on which CBO had based its estimates after the 2012 Supreme Court decision.[9]

The CMS projections also reveal how Medicaid costs would rise still more dramatically if all states were to participate in the full Medicaid expansion envisioned in the ACA. The CMS baseline estimate of $478 billion of federal Medicaid costs in 2021 translates to a total Medicaid cost of roughly $795 billion in that year (federal financing being 60 percent of the total). CMS projects that if all states participate in the ACA's Medicaid expansion, total program costs will rise still further in that year to roughly $831 billion.[10]

It is widely acknowledged that federal Medicaid costs are on an unsustainable trajectory, even apart from the issue of the ACA's Medicaid expansion.[11] Along with Medicare and Social Security, the new health coverage obligations arising under the ACA embody the main categories of federal spending projected to grow over the long term at rates faster than the federal tax base can sustain.[12] Accordingly, every recent and significant bipartisan discussion of how to best address the federal budget deficit has prompted proposals to reduce the rate of growth of federal Medicaid expenditures. The amount of savings envisioned in these various budget proposals varies significantly, but all reflect a shared bipartisan understanding that projected federal Medicaid cost growth will need to be scaled back.

EFFECTS OF MEDICAID EXPANSION ON STATE BUDGETS

The 2012 Supreme Court decision left states with the voluntary option of considerably expanding their Medicaid rolls to cover all childless adults with incomes effectively up to 138 percent of the FPL. In effect, the Medicaid expansion is an opportunity for states to significantly expand health benefits for their own citizens while passing the vast majority of the bill to federal taxpayers who mostly reside in other states. But at the same time, states will themselves face substantial additional costs if they choose to expand.

The expansion decision arrives at a time when state budgets are already under severe strain as a result of the recent recession as well as the mounting costs arising under Medicaid to date. Total state-financed Medicaid expenditures rose from roughly $31 billion in 1990 to roughly $157 billion in 2011, even though the federal share of total Medicaid costs had risen over the same period from 57 percent to 63 percent.[13] A survey of state budgets showed that already by 2011, state-financed Medicaid expenditures accounted for nearly 24 percent of state budgets.[14]

The fact that the federal government picked up 63 percent of total Medicaid costs in 2011 is significant for state decision making going forward. The percentage of total Medicaid costs financed from federal funds in that year was kept artificially high—and thus, state-financed expenditures held artificially low—as a result of temporary assistance provided to states through the 2009 federal stimulus law. In 2009, 2010, and 2011, effective federal financing assistance percentages averaged 65 percent, 67 percent, and 63 percent respectively, each annual percentage being substantially higher than the long-term average of 57 percent. As a result, even states that participate in the ACA's Medicaid expansion must actually finance a higher share of total Medicaid expenditures in the future than they did during the 2009–11 period, despite the generous federal financing assistance percentages promised under the ACA, as reflected in figure 2.[15]

Partially as a result of the expiration of temporary stimulus assistance, and partially as a result of rising caseload and general health care cost inflation, states face substantial Medicaid cost increases irrespective of their decisions about whether to expand Medicaid per

Figure 2. State Share of Total Medicaid Expenses (Compared to the 2009–11 Stimulus Period)

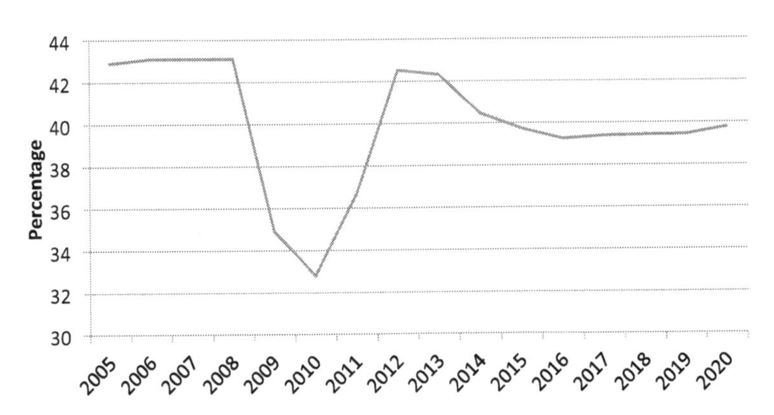

Source: Office of the Actuary, Centers for Medicare and Medicaid Services, "2012 Report on the Financial Outlook for Medicaid," 2012, table 3.

the terms of the ACA. Some estimates find that expansion would further increase state Medicaid costs by only roughly 3 percent, but this modest incremental increase would still create additional fiscal pressure at a particularly inopportune moment for states.[16] Current CMS estimates are that total state Medicaid costs will rise by 125 percent from 2010 to 2020 based on updated assumptions for partial state participation in the ACA's Medicaid expansion.[17] Even by Medicaid standards, this is an extremely rapid rate of cost growth, representing a substantial acceleration in state-financed costs relative to the 2000–10 period.[18]

Some advocates of expansion have argued that the ACA's generous promises of federal support for Medicaid expansion, combined with the fact that states currently face substantial costs for the treatment of the uninsured, together mean that states could actually save money by choosing to expand Medicaid. Although reducing the cost of treating the uninsured is an important factor to weigh as states contemplate Medicaid expansion, the available data do not appear to support the suggestion of net cost savings. On average, states should expect their total expenditures to rise significantly if they expand Medicaid.

A Henry J. Kaiser Foundation study found that roughly 33 percent of the cost of treating the uninsured is "uncompensated," with these costs in turn distributed between entities that include the federal government as well as state governments.[19] Taken together, the data suggest that roughly 10.6 percent of the total cost of treating the uninsured is financed by state governments. Taking into account the phenomenon under which individuals with insurance tend to purchase more health care services than those without, states on average would need to face no more than 8 percent of the cost of covering the newly Medicaid-insured in order to come out ahead fiscally.[20] In other words, an effective FMAP (federal medical assistance percentage) rate of 92 percent for the entire coverage expansion population would be required to allow expansion to be a fiscal gain for the states, on average.

Under the terms of the ACA, the federal government is promising to fund 90 percent of the cost of covering the newly eligible population from 2020 onward. This, however, substantially overstates the share of expansion costs that the federal government will actually pay, due largely to a phenomenon known as the "woodwork effect."

The woodwork effect is so called because it is expected that many people who were already eligible for Medicaid but had not previously signed up will emerge "out of the woodwork" to claim Medicaid benefits as coverage is expanded. This expectation is based in part on the ACA's outreach processes under which previously eligible individuals are to be enrolled in Medicaid if they attempt to sign up for the ACA's new health exchanges.[21] The ACA's imposition of a tax on those without health insurance is also expected to increase Medicaid enrollment among the eligible population. CBO estimates that roughly one-third of those with incomes below the FPL who receive Medicaid coverage under the ACA will be individuals who were eligible under prior law.[22]

Importantly, previously eligible individuals would not trigger federal support at the generous financing assistance rates of the ACA, but rather at the lower levels that existed in pre-ACA law. On average, the federal government has paid 57 percent of the cost of Medicaid coverage for those previously eligible. Putting all these numbers together, it should be expected that over the long term, states will need to shoulder roughly 21 percent of the cost of financing expanded Medicaid coverage for those in poverty. This is substantially more than the estimated break-even level of 8 percent.

The 21 percent figure is a rough average estimate of states' share of the added financing burden. Percentage financing burdens would vary significantly by state. States that historically have had higher uninsured percentages among those with incomes below the FPL, such as Texas, Nevada, and Montana, would likely experience proportional cost increases that are higher than this average.[23]

As states confront this decision, they must also factor in the previously mentioned consensus that the growth of federal Medicaid expenditures will need to be slowed. At this time, no person can state with certainty how much federal Medicaid expenditures will be reduced from current schedules, nor how much of these costs will be passed to states rather than embodying absolute reductions in the growth of total Medicaid costs. It would be unrealistic, however, for states to assume in their fiscal planning that federal expenditure schedules will be unchanging going forward.

INTERACTIONS BETWEEN PROVISIONS OF THE ACA

The particulars of the 2012 Supreme Court decision created unintended interactions between various provisions of the ACA, producing what appears to be a common incentive now facing all states: specifically, to decline to cover childless adults with incomes above the FPL under Medicaid.

This common incentive is an unintended consequence of the legislation's course first through Congress and later through the Supreme Court.[24] By original design, the ACA was intended to dramatically expand health coverage by a variety of methods. Individuals were to be subjected to a federal tax or penalty if they did not carry health insurance; employers (other than the smallest businesses) were generally to be assessed a penalty if they did not provide health insurance to their employees; states were to be required to cover childless adults with incomes of up to 138 percent of the FPL under Medicaid; and those with incomes between 100 and 400 percent of the FPL, if they lacked Medicaid coverage or an affordable employer offer of health insurance, were to be provided with substantial federal subsidies to purchase health insurance through the ACA's new exchanges.

These various features of the ACA were all intended to work in tandem. Federal subsidies for participants in the health exchanges were devised to be most generous for those with incomes between 100 and 133 percent of the FPL, effectively capping these low-income individuals' health insurance premiums in the exchanges at no more than 2 percent of their annual income.[25] But it was not expected that most such individuals would be drawing on these generous federal subsidies, given that states were required to cover those with incomes below 138 percent of FPL under Medicaid and that eligibility for the subsidies was extended only to those who were not otherwise Medicaid-eligible.[26]

This dynamic changed with the 2012 Supreme Court decision. Suddenly, states were no longer required to cover this population under Medicaid, leaving the subset of these individuals with incomes above the FPL potentially free to buy their health insurance through the exchanges with substantial federal support.

States have obvious financial incentives to have the federal government subsidize these individuals through the ACA's health exchanges. If the individuals are covered under Medicaid, states will eventually be required to finance 10 percent of the cost of their coverage under current law. If instead the individuals are covered through the exchanges, the entire subsidy would be financed by the federal government.[27]

The evidence further suggests that not only would declining to cover these individuals under Medicaid embody a cost savings for states, but that states could potentially provide the individuals with access to more generous health insurance through the exchanges, if they are left uninsured by Medicaid. Under 2012 CBO estimates, total average annual insurance value in 2022 for individuals in this income range would be roughly $9,500 in the exchanges, but less than $7,000 under Medicaid, with federal subsidies of roughly $9,000 in the exchanges and $6,000 under Medicaid.[28]

Taken together, these incentives suggest that leaving the population with incomes above the FPL uncovered by Medicaid is a win-win for states, delivering both cost savings as well as potentially more generous health coverage for their citizens. In recognition of this reality after the Supreme Court decision, CBO singled out 100 percent of the FPL as the income threshold at which states would lose their incentive to expand Medicaid:

> CBO anticipates that, instead of choosing to expand Medicaid eligibility fully to 138 percent of the FPL or to continue the status quo, many states will try to work out arrangements with the Department of Health and Human Services (HHS) to undertake partial expansions. For example, some states will probably seek to implement a partial expansion of Medicaid eligibility to 100 percent of the FPL, because, under the ACA, people below that threshold will not be eligible for subsidies in the insurance exchanges while people above that threshold will be if they do not have an offer of affordable coverage from an employer and meet other eligibility requirements.[29]

In the same report, CBO also projected that covering individuals only up to 100 percent FPL under Medicaid would be the most common choice made by states, although federal regulatory guidance was not then available as to whether states could make this partial-expansion choice. For their part, states perceived that their incentives pointed in this direction immediately after the Supreme Court decision. A letter sent by the National Governors Association just after the ruling on July 2, 2012, to HHS Secretary Kathleen Sebelius asked whether states that expanded up to 100 percent of FPL would still receive the ACA's enhanced federal assistance percentage.[30]

The aftermath of the Supreme Court decision displays the leverage of both sides in the federal–state discussion of the possible expansion of Medicaid. The federal government has the power to determine whether states are in compliance with Medicaid coverage requirements, and thus far has held to an interpretation that states must expand fully to 138 percent of the FPL to receive the enhanced federal assistance percentage under the ACA. At the same time, powerful incentives and leverage are pulling in the other direction. As we have seen, states have an enormous incentive to decline to cover those above 100 percent of the FPL under Medicaid, plus the federal government cannot force them to expand either fully or in part; the ultimate expansion decision rests with the states. Further shoring up the states' leverage, the language of the ACA specifies that its enhanced federal assistance percentage will be provided for any "newly eligible" recipient, defined in the statutory text as all those made eligible per the terms of the ACA who were not already eligible at the time the ACA was enacted.[31]

The interaction of these various provisions of the ACA with the recent Supreme Court decision creates a delicate balance of considerations, such that it is unsurprising that states are now making a wide range of decisions based in part on whether they believe they can negotiate satisfactory expansion terms in their discussions with HHS. This wide array of state coverage decisions reflects states' distinct value judgments and respective budgetary and demographic situations, but ultimately the incentives against covering those with incomes above 100 percent of FPL are powerful and appear to be common to all states. For the reasons discussed throughout this chapter, it is likely that with the passage of time and the continued escalation of Medicaid costs, an increasing number of states will conclude that it is in their interest for their citizens with incomes above the FPL to be covered through the health exchanges solely at federal expense.

CONCLUSION

The passage of the ACA in 2010 will dramatically increase total Medicaid expenditures, though how much of an increase will be a function of individual state decisions (many yet to be made) in the wake of the 2012 Supreme Court ruling. The Supreme Court rendered the ACA's expansion of Medicaid optional for states by striking down the federal government's ability to enforce it by withholding existing Medicaid funding. Federal Medicaid expenditures will rise sharply in the years ahead in any event, though far more dramatically to the extent that states choose to expand Medicaid coverage.

States' decisions about whether to expand Medicaid in the aftermath of the Supreme Court ruling are complex and closely balanced. Despite the arguments of some advocates that expanding Medicaid will reduce state costs of treating the uninsured, the available data do not appear to support the suggestion of net cost savings for states. On average, states should expect their total expenditures to rise significantly if they choose to expand Medicaid. These state expansion costs arise because their shares of Medicaid obligations for the expansion population are projected to significantly exceed savings with respect to their current costs of care for the uninsured. Such new costs of expansion would accrue at a time when Medicaid expenditures are already straining state budgets, on top of increasing baseline cost obligations that are a consequence of rising Medicaid caseloads, continuing health care cost inflation, and the wearing away of recent federal stimulus assistance.

Apparently common to all states is a disincentive to expand Medicaid to individuals with incomes above the FPL, as these individuals—if left uninsured by Medicaid—will be eligible for more generous coverage through the ACA's health exchanges with subsidies financed entirely by the federal government. With the passage of time and as general Medicaid costs rise, it appears likely that more states will feel compelled to respond to this incentive by limiting Medicaid coverage for childless adults solely to those with incomes below the FPL.

NOTES

1. Patient Protection and Affordable Care Act, Pub. L. No. 111-148, 124 Stat. 119 (2010) (codified as amended sections of 42 U.S.C.).
2. Office of the Actuary, Centers for Medicare and Medicaid Services, "2012 Report on the Financial Outlook for Medicaid" (Department of Health & Human Services, 2012), 2, http://medicaid.gov/Medicaid-CHIP-Program-Information/By-Topics/Financing-and-Reimbursement/Downloads/medicaid-actuarial-report-2012.pdf.
3. Social Security Act, 42 U.S.C. § 1396c, "Operation of State Plans," http://ssa.gov/OP_Home/ssact/title 19/1904.htm.
4. National Federation of Independent Businesses et al. v. Sebelius, 132 S. Ct. 2566 (2012).
5. The Advisory Board Company maintains a running tally of state participation decisions at http://www.advisory.com/Daily-Briefing/2012/11/09/MedicaidMap. As of May 24, 2013, this survey found that 26 states had indicated participation, 1 was leaning toward participation, 4 were pursuing an alternative model, 6 were leaning against participation, and 13 had declined to participate.
6. Congressional Budget Office, "CBO's May 2013 Estimate of the Effects of the Affordable Care Act on Health Insurance Coverage" (Washington, DC: Government Printing Office, May 2013), table 1, http://www.cbo.gov/sites/default/files/cbofiles/attachments/44190_EffectsAffordableCareActHealthInsuranceCoverage_2.pdf.
7. Congressional Budget Office, "CBO's May 2013 Estimate of the Effects of the Affordable Care Act on Health Insurance Coverage" (Washington, DC: Government Printing Office, May 2013), table 2, http://www.cbo.gov/sites/default/files/cbofiles/attachments/44190_EffectsAffordableCareActHealthInsuranceCoverage_2.pdf; Congressional Budget Office, "Medicaid Spending and Enrollment Detail for CBO's May 2013 Baseline," May 2013, http://www.cbo.gov/sites/default/files/cbofiles/attachments/44204_Medicaid.pdf.
8. Office of the Actuary, Centers for Medicare and Medicaid Services, "2012 Report on the Financial Outlook for Medicaid," table 3.
9. Congressional Budget Office, "Estimates for the Insurance Coverage Provisions of the Affordable Care Act Updated for the Recent Supreme Court Decision," July 2012.
10. Office of the Actuary, "2012 Report on the Financial Outlook for Medicaid," 39.
11. Charles Blahous, "The Affordable Care Act's Optional Medicaid Expansion: Considerations Facing State Governments" (Mercatus Research, Mercatus Center at George Mason University, Arlington, VA, March 5, 2013), 30–34, http://mercatus.org/publication/affordable-care-acts-optional-medicaid-expansion-considerations-facing-state-governments.
12. Congressional Budget Office, "The Long-Term Budget Outlook" (Washington, DC: Government Printing Office, June 2012), 13, http://www.cbo.gov/publication/43288: "Under CBO's two scenarios, the projected growth in noninterest spending as a share of GDP over the long term stems from increases in mandatory spending, particularly in outlays for the government's major health care programs: Medicare, Medicaid, the Children's Health Insurance Program (CHIP), and the insurance subsidies that will be provided through the exchanges created under the Affordable Care Act (ACA). Under both scenarios, total outlays for those health care programs would grow much faster than GDP, increasing from 5.4 percent of GDP in 2012 to about 10 percent in 2037."
13. Office of the Actuary, "2012 Report on the Financial Outlook for Medicaid," 2012,

table 3, http://medicaid.gov/Medicaid-CHIP-Program-Information/By-Topics/Financing-and-Reimbursement/Downloads/medicaid-actuarial-report-2012.pdf.

14. National Association of State Budget Officers (NASBO), "Budget Topics: Healthcare and Medicaid," http://www.nasbo.org/budget-topics/healthcare-medicaid. See also NASBO, "2010 State Expenditure Report," 2011, http://www.nasbo.org/sites/default/files/2010%20State%20Expenditure%20Report.pdf.
15. The most recent projection data presented in figure 2 reflect CMS assumptions with respect to state participation in the Medicaid expansion as made in Office of the Actuary, "2012 Report on the Financial Outlook for Medicaid," table 3. That the statement is true specifically for states that participate in the Medicaid expansion is further substantiated by Centers for Medicare and Medicaid Services, "2011 Actuarial Report on the Financial Outlook for Medicaid," table 3, which shows a similar pattern under the different assumption that all states participate in the expansion.
16. Blahous, "The Affordable Care Act's Optional Medicaid Expansion," 20.
17. Office of the Actuary, "2012 Report on the Financial Outlook for Medicaid," table 3.
18. From 2000 to 2010, state-financed Medicaid costs grew cumulatively by approximately 48 percent. Blahous, "The Affordable Care Act's Optional Medicaid Expansion," 18.
19. Jack Hadley and John Holahan, "The Cost of Care for the Uninsured," Kaiser Commission, May 2004, http://www.kff.org/uninsured/upload/the-cost-of-care-for-the-uninsured-what-do-we-spend-who -pays-and-what-would-full-coverage-add-to-medical-spending.pdf.
20. The aforementioned Kaiser study estimates that, if covered by Medicaid, these individuals' health care consumption would rise by roughly 39 percent. The full deviation of the 8 percent figure can be found in Blahous, "Affordable Care Act's Optional Medicaid Expansion," 26.
21. ACA, http://www.gpo.gov/fdsys/pkg/PLAW-111publ148/pdf/PLAW-111publ148.pdf.
22. Congressional Budget Office, "Estimates for the Insurance Coverage Provisions of the Affordable Care Act Updated for the Recent Supreme Court Decision," July 2012, http://www.cbo.gov/publication/43472.
23. Blahous, "The Affordable Care Act's Optional Medicaid Expansion," 27.
24. Some who have written about this history refer to this result more directly as a "mistake." See for example Dylan Scott, "The Story Behind the Biggest Mistake in Obamacare," *Governing.com*, February 2013, http://www.governing.com/blogs/fedwatch/gov-obamacare-mistake.html.
25. Health Care and Education Reconciliation Act of 2010, Pub. L. No. 111-152, § 1001 (2010).
26. Scott, "The Story Behind the Biggest Mistake in Obamacare." "The ACA stipulates that an individual can't qualify for both Medicaid *and* a tax subsidy (as people between 100 and 138 percent of the federal poverty level technically would). To address that gap, the ACA said that anyone who qualifies for both would just automatically be enrolled in Medicaid. So why don't the thresholds simply meet at 138 percent? Well, they were supposed to, but because of an oversight while the bill was being amended in the Senate, they don't. But it didn't matter as long as the Medicaid expansion was mandatory, which it was always supposed to be. But then the Supreme Court ruled last June that the expansion wasn't required—states could choose whether or not to expand Medicaid eligibility to 138 percent of the poverty line. That's an outcome no one saw coming, not even the people who wrote the law. By making the Medicaid

expansion optional, the Court exposed this obscure mistake that had been buried in 906 pages of legislation. And it created a huge loophole: In states that aren't expanding Medicaid, those 'in-betweeners'—residents who make between 100 and 138 percent of the poverty line—will now qualify for tax subsidies to buy private insurance instead. 'It was unintentional,' said one person who was involved in drafting the bill in the Senate. Like other sources interviewed for this story, this person spoke on condition of anonymity in order to speak candidly about the error and private deliberations around the ACA. 'This strange confluence of events got us here. Nobody thought the Supreme Court would rule as it did,' the source said. 'If the Medicaid expansion had occurred as we wrote it, then this wouldn't have mattered. The number of turns in the plot was hard to anticipate.'"

27. These subsidies consist essentially of federal tax credits; beyond direct subsidy costs, states could face other administrative and information technology costs in the exchanges depending on who sets them up and how they are administered.

28. For a fuller derivation of these figures, see Blahous, "The Affordable Care Act's Optional Medicaid Expansion."

29. Congressional Budget Office, "Estimates for the Insurance Coverage Provisions of the Affordable Care Act Updated for the Recent Supreme Court Decision," July 2012, http://www.cbo.gov/publication/43472.

30. Letter from the National Governors' Association to HHS Secretary Kathleen Sebelius, July 2, 2012, http://www.nga.org/cms/home/federal-relations/nga-letters/executive-committee-letters/col2-con tent/main-content-list/july-2-2012-letter---affordable.html. HHS's answer was effectively to say "no"; Letter from Secretary Kathleen Sebelius to governors, July 10, 2012, http://www.ncsl.org/documents /health/GovLetter7-10.pdf. However, HHS has subsequently allowed individual states to pursue proposals to effectively allow those above 100 percent of FPL to be enrolled in private insurance plans. See http://www.washingtonpost.com/blogs/wonkblog/wp/2013/02/28/arkansass-different-plan-to-expand-medicaid/.

31. Sections 1905 and 1902 of the Social Security Act, http://ssa.gov/OP_Home/ssact/title19/1905.htm and http://ssa.gov/OP_Home/ssact/title19/1902.htm.

CHAPTER 6: A PHYSICIAN'S PERSPECTIVE

DARCY NIKOL BRYAN, MD

Socioeconomic factors play a large role in health but historically have been mostly ignored by policymakers with a narrow focus on health care or worse, insurance access. Economic prosperity, neighborhood safety, environmental protection, educational opportunity, and income are all crucial determinants of people's health. By focusing on insurance and access, while failing to address these important socioeconomic factors, the passage of the Patient Protection and Affordable Care Act (ACA)[1] in March 2010 will have a limited influence on the health and well-being of Americans. Furthermore, the ACA's focus on measuring the process of health care delivery is no substitute for proper health outcome measurement.

As an obstetrician-gynecologist practicing in California's Inland Empire, I have the privilege of caring for a diverse population of women coming from a broad array of economic, cultural, and racial backgrounds. They are part of the population that, ostensibly, the ACA intends to help. Unfortunately, access to health insurance has a limited impact on overall population health, which is influenced by a variety of socioeconomic factors. Worse yet, the policies currently in place focus heavily on providing insurance, with little regard to access to health care or outcomes. There has been even less regard for the effect of these policies on the practice of medicine, and for the variety of unintended consequences that have been detrimental to the care of patients and provision of health care.

This chapter, with a preliminary sketch of the philosophical underpinnings of the debate that too often regards health care as a right, will briefly describe the history of Medicaid and the concomitant state program, Medi-Cal, that provides health insurance coverage for many of my patients, along with exploring other government attempts to expand health insurance. The sections that follow discuss the shortcomings of this focus on insurance, first describing my direct experiences as a physician. I then examine how the system sets up disincentives for cost containment and provokes overtreatment. The next section considers the tensions with respect to physician autonomy that were present when Medicaid and similar programs were created. Lastly, I discuss the fact that health insurance is a relatively small factor in health outcomes. It is critical that we shift focus to health outcomes and away from a narrowed focus on health insurance.

CONCEPTUAL TENSIONS

It is useful to briefly discuss why some policy makers support a strong governmental role in the health care marketplace, buttressing their arguments with claims of market failures. The philosophical roots of the quest for universal health coverage, the ACA, and the creation of the Medicaid program lie in the concept of a human right to health. Though this paper is not advocating that health care is a "right," it is nonetheless critical to understand the conceptual tension that exists because many people do believe that.

The United States has largely avoided the language of human rights in its efforts to reform its health care system, possibly because the Bill of Rights precisely denotes what is, and therefore what is not, a "right." The concept of rights springs up in public policy regularly (for example, the right to know what is in your food, the right to basic telecommunications). Nevertheless, human health as a right and the laws that subsequently arise from that basis are founded on two beliefs and concepts: (1) human rights are universal and immutable; and (2) human rights transcend state sovereignty and oblige governments to protect, respect, and fulfill the human rights of all people within their jurisdictions.[2] Historically, a human right to health was initially formalized within international law in Article 25 of the 1948 Universal Declaration of Human Rights (UDHR).[3] In the year 2000, the United Nations (UN) Committee on Economic, Social, and Cultural Rights drafted General Comment 14, which presents four elements key to achieving the right to health: availability, accessibility, acceptability, and quality.[4] Many ACA provisions address some of the criteria established by the United Nations for each of these key elements.[5] It is important to note that the United States has not ratified the United Nations' assertion of a human right to health. A logical outcome of the United Nations' concept is a single-payer health care system.[6]

Philosophically, there are two kinds of rights—negative and positive. Negative rights oblige inaction; in other words, others may not damage our health, take our private property, or inhibit freedom of speech. Positive rights entail a right to receive some good or service from another and involve correlative duties obliging provision of that good or service. The notion of a right to health care falls under the category of a positive right. Importantly, it is inherently controversial as to who is obliged to provide health care services. Jan Narveson asserts that there is no right to health care and that compelling someone else to pay for it through compulsory taxation is a right no one has. "It is a familiar contradiction of the welfare state to argue: 'Hey, this is such a good thing that of course you want it! Therefore, we will *make you take it.*' The conclusion is inconsistent with its premise."[7] Then there is the problem of distributive justice: how should health care be distributed once its provision is compelled? Should it be on the basis of need, merit, or strict equality?[8] Narveson states the following: "No one should be in the position that his fellows can exact payments from others for avoidable voluntary imposed risks."[9] Smoking, overeating, excessive alcohol intake and other high-risk lifestyle choices have completely foreseeable health consequences. Is it just to drain the financial resources of those who are willing to devote effort, time, and energy to maintaining their physical health in order to support those who do not care?

FROM MEDICAID TO THE AFFORDABLE CARE ACT

A desire to help the poor has resulted in the creation of a complex network of federal and state programs, with the ACA being the most recent and ambitious attempt to expand health insurance.

Medicaid's Historical Impact

Medicaid's enactment in the Social Security Amendments of 1965 mandated the coverage of certain categorical groups (e.g., poor families receiving cash assistance from the Aid to Families with Dependent Children). Its enactment arose out of the long struggle to adopt universal health insurance in the United States, affirming efforts by the federal government to bolster the public health infrastructure.[10] Since then, incremental expansion of the program has occurred with the view, by some policymakers, toward the creation of a path to more universal health care for Americans. Medicaid is to serve as a cornerstone beyond welfare medicine. Medicaid's instigation was built upon the Kerr-Mills program (1960–63), which offered broad health care benefits to the low-income elderly.[11] With the establishment of Medicaid, coverage was expanded to protect the blind, permanently disabled, and adults in mostly single-headed families and their dependent children.[12] Each state was given the discretion to determine the poverty level required to be eligible for the program. This resolution led to great variation in Medicaid's implementation across the country. The flexibility provided to the states was eventually limited by the Supplementary Security Income program of 1972, which joined state-run assistance programs for the elderly, blind, and disabled into one nationally uniform program with eligibility determined by a federal standard.[13]

Medicaid expansions to children, infants, and pregnant women increased gradually between 1984 and 1990, ultimately covering about five million children and 500,000 pregnant women across the United States.[14] This expansion was driven by the prodigious costs linked to the care of low birth weight (LBW) babies and their increased risk for multiple health problems throughout their lives. LBW infants, defined as a birth weight less than 2,500 grams (about 5.5 pounds), are at higher risk for high blood pressure, cerebral palsy, deafness, blindness, and lung disease, as well as behavioral problems and cognitive developmental problems.[15] Access to prenatal care was touted to make good economic sense because it was believed to lessen the incidence of LBW infants. For example, the expected costs of delivery and initial care of a baby weighing 1,000 grams at birth was greater than $100,000 in year 2000 dollars.[16] Eventually, Medicaid has come to finance about 40 percent of all births and has supported the creation of the modern neonatal intensive care unit.[17] During this time, increases in Medicaid expenditures occurred mainly through budget reconciliation bills, masking the program's expansion.[18] Meanwhile, state and federal health care spending for the poor increased from $75 billion in 1986 (in 1996 dollars) to almost $180 billion in 1996.[19] In 2011, federal and state Medicaid spending totaled almost $414 billion.[20]

Medicaid has facilitated the building of health care infrastructure in poor urban and rural communities. In doing so, health care providers and health insurers play a crucial role in gaining expansions of the program and opposing reductions.[21] The ACA furthers the expansion of Medicaid by presenting a federal option to cover any low-income adult under age 65 without regard to personal characteristics (e.g., disability, pregnancy). States can now choose to extend Medicaid to these adults with incomes at or below 133 percent of the federal poverty level (FPL). This establishes Medicaid as a platform for aiding coverage of more than 30 million uninsured Americans. Notably, through a series of landmark judicial decisions, some have come to view Medicaid as a social contract with individually enforceable legal entitlements and rights to care.[22] For those who view Medicaid as an individual right, this philosophical positioning can be seen in such initiatives as the community health centers program, the deinstitutionalization of health care provision through public health care centers, and the delivery of health care to children with special needs. When I was a medical school resident in California, the drop in obstetrical volume was notable as Medi-Cal patients were delivered in private hospitals away from the training hospitals that had traditionally supported indigent care. Access to "mainstream" health care became a perceived right.

The ACA's Impact on Medicaid

With the ACA's move toward using Medicaid as a means to ensure universal health care as sponsored by the federal government, federalism tensions have arisen as states fight the expansion. States have traditionally varied in their commitment to Medicaid, with some states being more administratively dexterous in enhancing participation rates, whereas others are much less flexible. The ACA, operating alongside Medicaid, is likely to create enormous administrative problems as fluctuating enrollee incomes will cause individuals to alternate between Medicaid and health exchange products.[23] States with low Medicaid participation rates are particularly threatened by the ACA because of the fact that residents currently eligible for Medicaid, but not enrolled, would be added to the program without triggering the federal government's generous matching payments. Additionally, the federal funding share for those newly eligible under ACA guidelines will decline to 90 percent by 2020, further threatening states' budgets. (For more on the ACA's implications for state budgets, see chapter 5, page 83.)

In 2011, California was at the top of the list of states for a budget shortfall, in the amount of $14.4 billion.[24] In the future, the effects of Medicaid expansion will be uniquely magnified in California by the large number of uninsured and undocumented immigrants living there. This group will comprise approximately 1.24 million people or 40 percent of those who will remain uninsured after ACA. Of the remainder of the uninsured who are not undocumented immigrants, 36 percent will be those subject to the individual mandate who will have chosen to remain uninsured, 13 percent are projected to be documented residents not subject to the mandate, and 11 percent will have had coverage but then lost it. Thirty-eight percent of the 3.77 million currently uninsured in California will be on public insurance in 2016;[25] a very large budgetary impact indeed!

Cost Containment Strategies in the ACA and Medicaid

Approximately half of the increase in health insurance provisions resulting from the ACA will be obtained through expansion of the Medicaid program and will account for an estimated 45 percent of the overall cost of reform.[26] Both public and private national spending on health care is projected to grow by 5.8 percent per year through 2020 according to the actuaries for the Centers for Medicare and Medicaid Services (CMS).[27] The federal and state governments together are estimated to spend about $3.4 billion more in providing public insurance to the formally uninsured.[28] Unfortunately, current cost-containment strategies are focused on reduction of federal health expenditures rather than creating the means for decreasing per capita spending on health care in the United States, which is more than twice that observed in other developed nations.[29]

As an example of federal cost-containment strategies, Section 3403 of the ACA has created the controversial "Independent Payment Advisory Board" (IPAB), which will recommend ways to reduce costs if the CMS chief actuary predicts that the per capita rate of growth for Medicare spending will exceed the "targeted rate."[30]

Under the law, IPAB recommendations are limited, and may not raise costs to beneficiaries, restrict benefits, or modify eligibility criteria.[31] Instead, the law directs IPAB's focus on Medicare Advantage Plans, Medicare Part D, skilled nursing facilities, home health, dialysis, ambulance services, ambulatory surgical centers, and durable medical equipment.[32]

Other ideas for reining in US medical care spending included in the ACA are policies promoting accountable care organizations (ACOs), primary care medical homes, bundled payment, pay for performance, comparative effectiveness research, and health information technology.[33] Secretary of Health and Human Services (HHS) Kathleen Sebelius stated that "every cost-cutting idea that every health economist has brought to the table is in this bill."[34] But systemwide, reliable cost control is lacking, with tepid reform a *realpolitik* necessity in order to get the ACA approved by the legislature.[35] At the same time, the Obama administration and congressional Democrats extracted more than $400 billion in projected savings out of Medicare, largely by reducing payments to hospitals and private insurers that operate as Medicare Advantage plans.[36] Decreasing reimbursement rates will likely threaten provider access. Ironically, the American Medical Association agreed to support the ACA after the US Congress promised to change the sustainable growth rate used to calculate updates to fee-schedule payments in Medicare.[37]

As James Capretta explains in chapter 7, another proposed federal budget cost-saving device is to shift the risk of Medicaid onto the states in the form of block grants. With block grants, the federal government would allot a fixed amount of dollars per capita to the states, which in turn would have more flexibility in determining Medicaid eligibility and benefits. Yet, as states face a budgetary Armageddon through increasing health care expenditures, many may choose to limit eligibility, leading to the same old problems of expensive emergency room care and minimal access to primary care, and no improvement in health outcomes.

FROM PHILOSOPHY TO PRACTICE: ONE PHYSICIAN'S EXPERIENCE

When I was a new graduate from the University of California at Los Angeles's OB/GYN residency program in 2004, I opted to practice in Riverside, having an affection and admiration for the hardworking people in California's Inland Empire, combined with an awareness of the region's great need for doctors. The Inland Empire encompasses Riverside and San Bernardino counties and is California's fastest-growing metropolitan area, driven by what economist John Husing has described as "dirt theory" (i.e., cheap land attracting growth through affordable housing).[38] The region has suffered for decades from slow economic growth, with a poor population supported mainly by agricultural work. The region I work in is what the Brookings Institution calls "the Third California," extending from the outer suburbs of Los Angeles to the Northern Californian foothills.[39] Composing the southern part of the Third California, Riverside and San Bernardino counties have 3.7 million residents. The population tends to be substantially less well educated than that of the coastal regions; 25 percent of those 25 or older have less than a high school degree.[40]

The Inland Empire has significant health problems linked to its challenging socioeconomic and environmental conditions. Its role as a transportation hub for the Los Angeles–Long Beach port complex has led to increased air pollution from heavy automobile and truck traffic corridors. Two-thirds or more of adults ages 18 and older in the region are overweight or obese, a source of much preventable disease and death.[41] Other health problems linked to poverty are also of concern. According to the University of Wisconsin Population Health Institute County Health Rankings, Riverside placed 27th and San Bernardino 44th in health outcomes out of 57 counties in California.[42]

As the "Third California" continues to grow rapidly (with a population of almost 10 million, greater than that of 42 states in the United States),[43] incredible strains will be placed on the region's existing health care infrastructure. Disturbingly, the Inland Empire has the worst shortage of physicians in California (about 40 primary care doctors and 70 specialists per 100,000 residents, approximately one-half the recommended primary care ratio).[44] As a physician, I am overwhelmed by these numbers and the thought of so many needing care. This insupportable provider shortage, which will likely worsen under the ACA, probably will lead to even greater delay in health care, ranging from longer wait times, poor access to providers, and an increased quantity of emergency department visits. Although the expansion of Medicaid through the ACA of 2010 is projected to increase insurance coverage, accounting for one-third of the overall growth in insurance coverage, the gap between the number of available doctors and patients will be exacerbated. Notably, only one-half of existing primary care physicians accepted new Medi-Cal (California's Medicaid) patients during 2008.[45] However, as will be discussed later, access to providers is far from the most important issue in health for this population.

As an obstetrician, I take care of pregnant women covered by Medi-Cal. Yet, sometimes I have felt alone in the care of these high-need patients, since Medi-Cal, as it currently stands, covers only obstetrical aspects of medicine. As an example, I recall a lovely stay-at-home mom who came to me for care early in her third pregnancy. Later, at the end of her first trimester, she started to randomly lose consciousness for short periods throughout the day. The work-up for loss of consciousness, however, is quite comprehensive. It is *not in the field of obstetrics* as it requires comprehensive evaluation of the heart and the brain. As a specialist in a multidisciplinary clinic, I knew only obstetricians and pediatricians took Medi-Cal insurance. I had no access to colleagues in neurology or cardiology who might provide their expertise to my patient, because Medi-Cal simply did not provide them with adequate reimbursement for their services. Subsequently, I had to transfer her to a county hospital, disrupting care continuity and adding stress to the patient and her family. Such are the vagaries of our current system.

COST OF MEDICINE

Why is medicine so expensive? Culturally, the western biomedical model framing disease as an invader to be defeated is the foundation of modern medicine and explains much about the typical physician's restricted focus on intervention. Additionally, the incentive system doctors face through reimbursement formulas explains a lot of the growth in the costs of health care. The scientific and positivistic approach to medicine has in many ways launched the modern medical–industrial complex, fostering a business model of high-cost health care delivery that does not match social needs. Large, extremely specialized, capital-intensive institutions have been created with the resulting neglect of less-costly primary and chronic care.[46] According to the book *Medicine and Culture*,[47] the American emphasis on aggressive medicine (compared with that of our European colleagues) is rooted in our cultural predilection for bold action and acute care over contemplation and judicious intervention that waits for solid empirical evidence of treatment efficacy.

In my own field of obstetrics and gynecology, American obstetricians often embrace technology with little evidence as to efficacy. The reasons behind this are a complex mixture of cultural attitudes, economic incentives to perform procedures, and professional liability concerns.[48] For example, maintenance tocolytics (uterine muscle relaxants) used to treat preterm uterine contractions have not been found to prevent prematurity or reduce perinatal mortality, yet many obstetricians still use them. Antenatal nonstress tests (NSTs) are routinely ordered for women considered to be at increased risk for stillbirth without significant evidence of efficacy.[49] The rate at which labor is induced increased from 9.5 percent to 21.2 percent between 1990 and 2004 in the United States, despite little evidence of clinical benefit,[50] and the national Cesarean-section (C-section) rate has increased from 20.7 percent to 30.2 percent from 1996 to 2005.[51] Unnecessary induction of labor and C-sections add significantly to the cost of care. Much of physician reimbursement is still driven by procedure (Current Procedural Terminology, or CPT, codes). In other words, health care providers must *do* something for higher compensation. As for professional liability, when was the last time an obstetrician was sued for ordering too many fetal ultrasounds or monitoring her patient too closely with NSTs? We are always criticized for not performing a C-section in a *timely* fashion, rarely for performing an *unnecessary* one.

The modern medical–industrial complex in the United States is notoriously poor at calculating and controlling cost; using opaque byzantine reimbursement formulas that lack transparency even to many health care executives. Costs are allocated to procedures, departments, and services based on payer reimbursement, not on the actual resources used to deliver care.[52] Kaplan and Porter eloquently state that "without proper measurement, the healthy dynamic of competition—in which the highest-value providers expand and prosper—breaks down. Instead, we have a zero-sum competition in which health care providers destroy value by focusing on highly reimbursed services, shifting costs to other entities, or pursuing piecemeal and ineffective line-item cost reductions."[53] They go on to assert that in order to manage value (patient outcomes achieved per dollar expended), both outcomes and cost must be measured at the patient level. This requires careful measurement of costs over a complete cycle of individual patient care for a particular medical condition. Most institutions are not administratively equipped to do this. Instead, providers measure only particular interventions they control, focusing on evidence-based guidelines and care processes.[54] Process measurement is no substitute for outcome measurement. Porter defines three tiers to outcome measurements most relevant to patients: (1) health status achieved or retained; (2) process of recovery; and (3) sustainability of health. Having feedback on patient outcomes leads to innovation in care and lessens cost.[55]

Another barrier thought to limit cost containment in health care is moral hazard due to insurance distorting health care markets. Having health insurance is believed to lead to excessive consumption of health care goods because insured individuals will consume medical services past the point at which the marginal utility of an additional service is equal to its marginal cost.[56] This prevents optimal pricing.

Under the current reimbursement environment stimulated by the ACA, groups of providers are consolidating within the US market at an accelerated rate, with multispecialty group practices or hospitals buying smaller practices and forming regional monopolies.[57] Such super groups will have a robust advantage in rate negotiations. Hospitals affiliated with a system and hospitals in very concentrated markets typically have higher charges and profits.[58] States, in turn, are outsourcing Medicaid to managed Medicaid plans, whose contracts are further fueling consolidation as commercial insurers buy their way into the market or make acquisitions to increase their market share and achieve economies of scale.[59] Medicaid managed care capitation rates are linked to fee-for-service (FFS) historical rates and must be high enough to attract commercial participants.[60] State officials assert that privatizing Medicaid through managed care leads to decreased cost and improvement in quality of care. This assumption has increased the percentage of Medicaid recipients enrolled in health maintenance organizations and other forms of Medicaid managed care from 11 to 71 percent from 1991 to 2009.[61] A recent study by Duggan suggests that shifting Medicaid recipients from FFS to managed care did not, on average, reduce Medicaid spending.[62] The data on quality of Medicaid managed care is also mixed. Aizer et al. studied pregnant women in California and found that those in Medi-Cal managed care received fewer prenatal visits and delivered fewer healthy babies than patients in the traditional Medicaid program.[63]

Consolidation has also been stimulated by payment reform efforts through ACO contracts established between CMS and ACOs. Providers that meet quality standards are eligible to share savings with Medicare. So far, CMS has contracts with approximately 250 ACOs covering four million Medicare beneficiaries.[64] The goal is to move from FFS payment to models supporting provider integration, care coordination, and patient education within a "medical home." But as organizations consolidate, costs will increase through greater bargaining power in regional markets. And as Porter has shown, our current assessment of value is deeply flawed. The imprecise quality metrics proposed to resolve this problem are unlikely to lead to improved health outcomes.

PHYSICIANS' RESPONSE TO MEDICAID

The forces that drive costs up in medicine also play a role in distorting physicians' incentives in other ways, as their autonomy is limited, affecting how they practice medicine. Historically, individual physicians have treated a certain amount of uninsured patients in their practice without charge or for a reduced fee as part of the medical profession's ethical obligation to care for the poor. With the advent of Medicare and Medicaid in 1965, what had been private nonsystematized volunteer work by doctors and charitable organizations shifted to a broader social responsibility embodied in public insurance. These programs subsidized physicians' ability to care for the indigent and needy. They also profoundly transformed American medicine at the socioeconomic level, making medicine dependent on social institutions and recasting it as a profession.[65]

The federal government's attempt to seek control over the cost of medicine stimulated by Medicare and Medicaid funding inaugurated the era of managed care in the 1970s, leading to the loss of medicine's independent professional and moral identity and altering the physician's relationship with his or her patient. Jotterand states the following: "Cost containment appeared suddenly as a *moral obligation* imposed on the physician. This means that the physicians are no longer exclusively committed to their patients but also dependent on and controlled by the social institutions that structure health care, in particular its economic aspects."[66]

Physicians' real incomes have been largely stagnant since the 1990s and have even declined in the past 10 years with the rapid expansion of managed care and private insurers adopting Medicare's physician fee schedule as a benchmark in negotiating payment rates.[67] If Medicaid is to be an effective cornerstone of health care reform, doctors will need to be fully on board. The most obvious barrier to physician acceptance is the typically low reimbursement levels offered by Medicaid for physician services. States have broad scope in setting physician reimbursement rates, causing Medicaid fees to vary much more widely than Medicare fees. In many states, Medicaid pays only about one-third of what Medicare pays for the same service.[68] Data from the National Center for Health Statistics on the use of office-based physician care imply that higher Medicaid fees increase the number of private physicians in medical and surgical specialties accepting Medicaid patients.[69]

Sommers et al. examined primary care physicians' willingness to see Medicaid patients by sampling 1,460 primary care providers (PCPs) who worked in an outpatient setting from the 2008 Center for Studying Health System Change Health Tracking Physician Survey, supplemented by 15 in-depth telephone interviews.[70] The study found that PCPs who were already serving a high volume of Medicaid patients were most likely to take on new Medicaid patients. Four out of 10 of these PCPs work in hospital-based practices and community health centers, tending to practice in lower-income areas. Practices based in hospitals can provide extra personnel, such as residents; and administrative efficiency, like centralized billing, that subsidize primary care provision to the poor. In addition, many Medicaid enrollees live in areas more likely to be served by community health centers and public hospitals (e.g., the inner city) than by office-based physician practices.[71] PCPs that practice in higher-income areas tended to take few or no Medicaid patients, citing low reimbursement, difficulty arranging specialist care, burden of dealing with psychosocial issues of poverty, and administrative hassles with Medicaid billing requirements.

Notably in the Sommers et al. study, Medicaid reimbursement fee levels are only one of many factors affecting the number of physicians willing to accept Medicaid patients. If increasing patient access to physicians is to be achieved, simple fee increases alone will not be enough to expand physician supply. Cunningham and Nichols examined the effects of Medicaid reimbursement on access to care of

Medicaid enrollees and found other determinants had a strong influence as well, including practice type, the extent of Medicaid managed care penetration in a particular geographical region, and the racial and ethnic composition of physicians and their communities.[72]

In addition to practice type, difficulty in coordinating care for Medicaid patients is another barrier to physician participation. Organizations having a large Medicaid population achieve the most effective health results, given their familiarity with the patients' special needs and their having an existing infrastructure for psychosocial support. Problems in disease management in the indigent patient population are further exacerbated by patients fluctuating between insured and uninsured status, resulting in loss of care continuity. Many in this population have difficulty communicating because of phone access, language barriers, illiteracy, and disability. One proposed method for quality improvement in Medicaid care is the creation of disease management programs dealing with chronically ill enrollees. As is well recognized, 50 percent of total health care spending is due to 25 percent of the population that has heart disease, diabetes, asthma, and hypertension.[73] Two major models exist for Medicaid chronic disease management programs. One is a primary care–focused action plan built on the chronic care model with participation by Federally Qualified Health Centers. The other is state investment in private disease management vendors.[74] The difficult goal of disease management programs is to improve health status by reducing unnecessary hospitalizations, increase primary care utilization, and improve medication compliance and patient self-management skills.

A later analysis by Cunningham and Hadley[75] led to some startling conclusions. The percent of physicians providing any charity care fell significantly from 76.3 percent in 1996–97 to 68.2 percent in 2004–05 and a growing number of doctors are receiving no income from Medicaid or are not accepting new Medicaid patients. This is likely secondary to further erosion of physician autonomy. Physicians are shifting to larger practices or institutional settings in order to gain the following: (1) leverage in negotiating with health plans; (2) economies of scale to counteract the increasing administrative and regulatory requirements of practicing medicine; (3) financial security through salaried positions; and (4) higher quality of life with a more flexible work schedule. Interestingly, being part of a large group prohibits individual physician decision making in providing charitable care (i.e., free care) against organizational policy, but large group membership improved the likelihood of physician acceptance of Medicaid. Autonomous physicians who owned their own practices were oppositely aligned and more likely to provide charity care and less likely to accept Medicaid. Cunningham and Hadley conclude, "free care will become increasingly concentrated in safety net providers—such as public hospitals and community health centers. . . . Unless steps are taken to reduce the number of uninsured, safety net providers are likely to be overwhelmed by this increasing concentration of care at their facilities, and as a consequence, more uninsured patients will not receive any care at all."[76] Loss of physician professional autonomy leads to an erosion of traditional physician professional values, such as free care for the poor. And poverty is a critical factor when it comes to health.

POVERTY'S IMPACT ON HEALTH

A family's income level is associated with morbidity and premature infant mortality, both internationally and within the United States.[77] Important and modifiable risk factors can be discovered and addressed during prenatal care visits, thereby improving pregnancy outcomes. In the late 1980s, rising concern about the United States' high infant mortality rate, compared with that of other industrialized countries, prompted passage of federal laws expanding Medicaid coverage for pregnant women. California thus followed suit by implementing several health policies aimed at increasing prenatal insurance coverage and utilization of care.[78] To understand the magnitude of Medi-Cal, it is useful to know that one out of every eight babies in the United States is born in California.[79] Throughout the 1980s and 1990s, California expanded Medi-Cal coverage to pregnant women by: (1) extending public insurance to undocumented foreign-born women; (2) increasing income eligibility from 110 to 200 percent of the FPL; and (3) eliminating the assets test for women with incomes below 200 percent of FPL. Additionally, barriers to prenatal care coverage were addressed by: (1) increasing payments to obstetric providers by 85 percent; (2) implementing continuous eligibility throughout the pregnancy; (3) shortening the Medi-Cal application form; and (4) instituting presumptive eligibility, allowing temporary but immediate coverage for women who believe they are eligible for Medi-Cal.[80] In response to concerns about fraud as Medi-Cal coverage expanded, the state created the California's Department of Health Care Services' antifraud program and implemented the annual Medi-Cal Payment Error Study in 2004.[81]

Following statewide policy changes, studies were done to assess the impact of increased access to prenatal care through expansion of Medi-Cal. For example, Braveman et al. conducted a cross-sectional postpartum survey of 3,071 low-income women with Medi-Cal or private coverage throughout pregnancy in California from 1994 to 1995. This was accomplished in order to identify critical noninsurance barriers to timely prenatal care.[82] Of those women, 28 percent had late prenatal care (e.g., the first health care provider visit occurred after 13 weeks of pregnancy). The following prepregnancy factors, beyond the reach and impact of publicly supported programs for pregnant women, were found to be the most important risk factors for untimely prenatal care: (1) unwanted or unplanned pregnancy; (2) no regular health care provider before pregnancy; (3) education at or below high school level; and (4) transportation problems. Another study performed by Nothnagle et al. investigated risk factors for late or no prenatal care after the expansion of Medi-Cal.[83] A statewide postpartum survey of 6,364 women delivering in California hospitals from 1994 to 1995 was conducted and found that absolute poverty (at or below the FPL) was associated with a ninefold increased risk of no prenatal care after adjusting for insurance, age, parity, marital status, ethnicity, and other significant potential barriers.[84] The authors surmised that women in absolute poverty were socially marginalized, therefore did not enroll in Medi-Cal and obtain prenatal care because they lived in a family or community unsupportive of prenatal care. Nearly 29 percent of women surveyed who had no prenatal care before delivery reported that their receiving prenatal care had not been very important to those close to them.[85]

Despite the value of prenatal care on an individual basis, the short time these women in poverty spend with a health care provider can be like a Band-Aid on the gaping wound of harsh daily life. I have pregnant patients who work in factories with no air-conditioning or long hours in retail with little job security. Telling them to sit down or hydrate when having uterine irritability must seem straight out of fantasy-land for them.

As those in population health sciences already recognize, the social and environmental determinants of health are critically important demanding a move beyond the narrow focus on access to health care. Illuminating this point further, Kindig et al. found that female mortality rates rose in 42.8 percent of US counties from 1992 to 2006.[86] The authors sampled 3,140 counties (or county equivalents), compiling data from County Health Rankings, the Behavioral Risk Factor Surveillance Survey, and the Centers for Disease Control and Prevention's compressed mortality database. The county-level percentage change in all-cause, age-adjusted mortality rate per 100,000 residents ages 75 or under for two time periods, 1992–96 and 2002–06, were examined. The authors used regression analysis to examine which county-level factors were associated with changes in mortality rates for males and females during this timeframe. Interestingly, none of the medical care factors (e.g., rates of primary care providers, preventable hospitalizations, percentage of uninsured) predicted changes in male or female mortality.[87] Geography had the strongest association with female mortality rates. Counties in the South and the Western United States had 6 percent higher female mortality rates than those in the Northeast.[88] Kindig et al. provided further evidence with this analysis that socioeconomic factors, such as education levels and rates of children living in poverty, have an equally strong or stronger association with county mortality rates compared to access to medical care (no perceived impact) or individual behavior (e.g., smoking rates having some impact).

America's Health Rankings has established four health determinant categories with weights of factors impacting health assigned by an expert panel as follows: 36 percent personal behaviors (somewhat contradictory to the Kindig et al. study); 25 percent community environment; 18 percent public and health policies; and 21 percent clinical care.[89] The University of Wisconsin along with the Robert Wood Johnson Foundation has used the following weights of health factors in their county health rankings: 40 percent social and economic factors; 30 percent health behaviors; 20 percent clinical care; and 10 percent physical environment.[90] Although the exact weights of the socioeconomic factors may not be precise, the implications for addressing health are clear. They count, and perhaps much more than clinical care. Certainly intrinsic or individual biological factors affecting health, such as genes, age, and sex, cannot be altered. Yet, economic conditions are modifiable and have a critical influence as well. These factors are outside the typical realm of physicians and are rarely addressed by hospitals, health plans, or even the public health community to a deep and meaningful extent. Economic prosperity, neighborhood safety, environmental issues, educational opportunity, and income all are crucial determinants of a region's morbidity and mortality. In sum, "place matters,"[91] as has been seen in the recent region-specific rise in female mortality in the United States. As a physician who has devoted her life to the health and well-being of women, I find it discouraging that clinical care has only a 20 percent impact for all that effort. Yet, doctors inherently focus on individual patients and their needs. This is both our strength and our evident loss of effectiveness.

The problem with focusing exclusively on health care access is that it ignores socioeconomic factors. As Evans and Stoddart have stated, "The concern is rather that the remaining shortfalls, the continuing burden of illness, disability, distress, and premature death, are less and less sensitive to further extensions in health care—we are reaching the limits of medicine. At the same time the evidence is growing in both quantity and quality that this burden may be quite sensitive to interventions and structural changes outside the health care system."[92] The importance of income levels on mortality is well recognized, with Peter Muening et al. estimating that Americans living on incomes less than 200 percent of the FPL claimed more than 400 million quality adjusted life-years (number of years of life that would be added by intervention) between 1997 and 2002, compared with those living on incomes 200 percent or more of the FPL.[93] This statistic is greater in impact than tobacco use and obesity.[94] Education levels also have a huge effect on health. Adults who do not have a high school diploma or GED are three times more likely than those with a college education to die before age 65. Every additional year in educational attainment reduces the odds of dying by 1 to 3 percent.[95]

Because of the relative importance of these other factors, the ACA quite obviously will have only a limited influence on the health and well-being of Americans. As has been demonstrated, access to health care providers and institutions is not the main issue in population health. Notably, the ACA does not take a public health approach in focusing on deficiencies in the United States health system, but rather attends to issues of health insurance.[96] However, if national health outcomes and improvement are lightly weighed in the balance, the policy ramifications of the law are quite notable. As a consequence of the ACA, eligibility will be expanded to cover individuals making a higher income and eliminate restrictions to allow for coverage of everyone with incomes under the specified level, not just the categorically eligible.[97] Interestingly, while trying to increase access to health care providers, the ACA seeks to contain costs related to health care expenditures by reducing payments to certain health plans and providers accepting Medicaid. The effectiveness of this approach has serious limitations. If cost restraints imposed are too harsh, physicians and hospitals will be forced to opt out of public insurance, an effect precisely the opposite of the one intended.

CONCLUSION

The essential question is, how can we ever achieve adequate health care with so many layers of need and at such crippling cost? The problems are real, immense, and complex. The United States spends ever-increasing sums of money for marginal benefits at best. Too much medical intervention can be unnecessary, possibly harmful, and without good scientific evidence as health care provision focuses on processes, not outcomes. The business model of the medical–industrial complex is opaque and notoriously complex with no clear link between price and value. Physicians are overwhelmed and dispirited as they see their time, which should be devoted to caring for patients, consumed by bureaucratic hurdles, multiplying regulations, and diminishing compensation. In vast numbers, doctors are shedding their traditional autonomy and becoming disempowered employees by merging their practices into corporate medicine. Medicine will be and has been diminished as a vital profession.

To understand these unwholesome phenomena, we should pull back the conceptual lens and look at the definition of health care. If you ask most people how they would want to spend their money or time, being in a medical center or hospital is at the bottom of the list. Our personal idea of health and well-being is different from health care. Well-being encompasses work that satisfies and sustains, having respect and support from friends and family, clean air and green vistas, safe neighborhoods to call home, and much more. To view the body narrowly as a machine with parts that needs to be fixed misses the critical ramifications of well-being on physical health. Concepts as nebulous as stress and despair rumble beneath the statistical surface as we see mortality rates layered along socioeconomic levels.

Yet the scientific biomedical model of health fosters the notion that well-being can somehow be obtained (purchased?) in a doctor's office or hospital. Within this philosophical framework, modern societies devote ever-increasing proportions of economic resources to health care. As is clear from the amplifying focus on cost containment, health care is not free. It requires a major commitment in time, energy, skills—and capital. Advances in medical technology and interventions have made huge strides in prolonging life and combating disease. But this is not the full picture. Population mortality is linked to levels of social support, stress, and powerlessness in very fundamental ways. Scholars categorize the four determinants of health as lifestyle, environment, human biology, and health care organization. Health care is only one component.

As a nation, we must ask ourselves if our unsustainable commitment of economic resources to health care is making us less healthy as a country. The solution will not come by devoting more time or intellectual energy on fixing the health care system. One hundred percent of governmental effort going toward 20 percent of the problem is a fatal sort of blindness. By impoverishing ourselves and our nation on health care expenditures, are we not neglecting the vital elements that are maintaining our health and well-being? State and federal budgets consumed with paying medical bills cannot fund, for example, education, environmental protection, or the creation of safe neighborhoods. Money dedicated to health care simply cannot be spent elsewhere.

NOTES

1. Patient Protection and Affordable Care Act, Pub. L. No. 111-148, 124 Stat. 119 (2010) (codified as amended sections of 42 U.S.C.).
2. Lance Gable, "The Patient Protection and Affordable Care Act, Public Health, and the Elusive Target of Human Rights," *Journal of Law, Medicine, & Ethics* 39, no. 3 (2011): 347.
3. United Nations General Assembly, *Universal Declaration of Human Rights*, December 10, 1948, 217 A (III), http://www.un.org/en/documents/udhr/index.shtml#a25.
4. http://www2.ohchr.org/english/bodies/cescr/comments.htm (last visited 05/25/2013).
5. Gable, "The Patient Protection and Affordable Care Act," 348.
6. Mary Crowley, "Justice as a Frame for Health Reform," *Hastings Center Report* 38, no. 1 (2008): 3.
7. Jan Narveson, "The Medical Minimum: Zero," *Journal of Medicine & Philosophy* 36, no. 6 (2011): 563.
8. Ronald Duska, "On the Rights to Health Care and Health Insurance." *Journal of Financial Service Professionals* 62, no. 1 (2008): 14–15.
9. Narveson, "The Medical Minimum," 568.

10. Colleen Grogan and Eric Patashnik, "Between Welfare Medicine and Mainstream Entitlement: Medicaid at the Political Crossroads," *Journal of Health Politics, Policy & Law* 28, no. 5 (2003): 824.
11. Ibid., 825.
12. Ibid.
13. Jill Quadagno, "From Old-Age Assistance to Supplemental Security Income: The Political Economy of Relief in the South, 1935–1972," in *The Politics of Social Policy in the United States*, ed. Margaret Weir, Ann Shola Orloff, and Theda Skocpol (Princeton, NJ: Princeton University Press, 1988).
14. Sara Rosenbaum, "Medicaid Expansions and Access to Health Care," in *Medicaid Financing Crisis: Balancing Responsibilities, Priorities, and Dollars*, ed. Diane Rowland, Judith M. Feder, and Alina Salganicoff (Washington, DC: AAAS Press, 1993).
15. Douglas Almond, Kenneth Chay, and David Lee, "The Costs of Low Birth Weight," *Quarterly Journal of Economics* 120, no. 3 (2005): 1031–32.
16. Ibid., 1031.
17. David Smith and Judith Moore, "Medicaid Politics and Policy: 1965–2007," *Journal of Health Politics, Policy and Law* 34, no. 3 (2009): 419.
18. Grogan and Patashnik, "Between Welfare Medicine and Mainstream Entitlement," 831.
19. R. Shep Melnick, "The Unexpected Resilience of Means-Tested Programs," Paper presented at the American Political Science Association Conference, Atlanta, September 2–5, 1999.
20. Henry J. Kaiser Family Foundation, *State Health Facts*, http://kff.org/medicaid /state-indicator/total-medicaid-spending/.
21. Smith and Moore, "Medicaid Politics and Policy," 418–19.
22. Smith and Moore, "Medicaid Politics and Policy," 421.
23. Frank Thompson, "The Medicaid Platform: Can the termites Be Kept at Bay?," *Journal of Health Politics, Policy and Law* 36, no .3 (2011): 551.
24. "Medicaid—Growth from Higher Penetration of a Growing Pie," in Black Book—*Obamacare, or How I Learned to Stop Worrying & Love Managed Care* (Bernstein Global Wealth Management, April 2011), 98, http://search.ebscohost.com/direct .asp?db=bth&jid=BMSA&scope=site.
25. Peter Long and Jonathan Gruber, "Projecting the Impact of the Affordable Care Act on California," *Health Affairs* 30, no. 1 (2011): 65–66.
26. Renee Landers and Patrick Leeman, "Medicaid Expansion Under the 2010 Health Care Reform Legislation: The Continuing Evolution of Medicaid's Central Role in American Health Care," *NAELA Journal* 7, no. 1 (2011): 144–45.
27. Caryl Carpenter, "Medicare, Medicaid, and Deficit Reduction," *Journal of Financial Service Professionals* 65, no. 6 (2011): 27.
28. Long and Gruber, "Projecting the Impact of the Affordable Care Act on California," 67.
29. OECD Health Data 2006: Statistics and Indicators for 30 Countries, http://www.oecd .org/health/health-systems/36960035.pdf.
30. Sarah Fontenot, "Will Health Care Costs Come Down? Watch the IPAB," *Physician Executive Journal of Medical Management* 39, no. 3 (2013): 84.

31. T. S. Jost, "The Independent Medicare Advisory Board," *Yale Journal of Health Policy, Law and Ethics* 11, no. 1 (2013).

32. Fontenot, "Will Health Care Costs Come Down?," 85.

33. Jonathan Oberlander, "Throwing Darts: American's Elusive Search for Health Care Cost Control," *Journal of Health Politics, Policy & Law* 36, no. 3 (2011): 477.

34. D. Gregory, K. Sebelius, O. Hatch, H. Ford Jr, E. J. Dionne, and R. Lowry, *Meet the Press*, March 7 broadcast, transcript March 11 (2010), http://www.msnbc.com/id/35727484/.

35. Oberlander, "Throwing Darts," 478.

36. Ibid., 479.

37. Miriam Laugesen, "Civilized Medicine: Physicians and Health Care Reform," *Journal of Health Politic, Policy & Law* 36, no. 3 (2011): 507–12.

38. Joel Kotkin and William Frey, "The Third California: The Golden State's New Frontier," *Brookings Institution Research Brief* (March 2007): 10.

39. Ibid., 1.

40. Ibid., 7.

41. Carolyn Mendez-Luck, Hongjian Yu, Ying-Ying Meng, Mona Jhawar, and Steven Wallace, "Too Many California Adults Are Tipping the Scales at an Unhealthy Weight," UCLA Center for Health Policy Research, April 1, 2005, http://escholarship.org/uc/item/06g4b176.

42. Robert Wood Johnson Foundation and the University of Wisconsin Population Health Institute, "County Health Rankings & Roadmaps," http://www.countyhealthrankings.org/app/california/2013/rankings/outcomes/overall/by-rank.

43. Kotkin and Frey, "The Third California," 2.

44. Annie Lowrey and Robert Pear, "Doctor Shortage Likely to Worsen with Health Law," *New York Times*, July 28, 2012, http://www.nytimes.com/2012/07/29/health/policy/too-few-doctors-in-many-us-communities.html?_r=0.

45. Kevin Grumbach and Andrew B. Bindman, "Physician Participation in Medi-Cal, 2008," Sacramento Briefing, California Health Care Foundation, March 26, 2010.

46. Barbara Perkins, "Designing High-Cost Medicine: Hospital Surveys, Health Planning, and the Paradox of Progressive Reform," *American Journal of Public Health* 100, no. 2 (2010): 223.

47. Lynn Payer, *Medicine and Culture: Revised Edition* (New York: Henry Holt and Company, 1996).

48. Charles Lockwood, "Obstetrics and Culture," *Contemporary OB/GYN* 52, no. 8 (2007): 8–11.

49. N. Pattison and L. McCowan, "Cardiotography for Antepartum Fetal Assessment," *Cochrane Database Syst Review* 2 (2000): CD001066.

50. J. A. Martin et al., "Births: Final Data for 2004," *National Vital Statistics Reports* 55, no. 1 (2006): 1–101.

51. B. E. Hamilton, J. A. Martin, and S. J. Ventura, "Births: Preliminary Data for 2005," *National Vital Statistics Reports* 55, no. 11 (2006): 1–18.

52. Robert Kaplan and Michael Porter, "How to Solve the Cost Crisis in Health Care," *Harvard Business Review* 89, no. 9 (2011): 46–64.

53. Ibid.
54. Michael Porter, "What Is Value in Health Care?," *NEJM* 363, no. 26 (2010): 2477–81.
55. Ibid., 2478–79.
56. Martin Gaynor, "Are Invisible Hands Good Hands? Moral Hazard, Competition, and the Second-Best in Health Care Markets," *Journal of Political Economy* 108, no. 5 (2000): 993.
57. Matt Bolch, "Costs Drive Medicaid's Reality," *Managed Health Care Executive* 23, no. 2 (2013): 27.
58. Robert Dowless, "The Health Care Cost-Shifting Debate: Could Both Sides Be Right?," *Journal of Health Care Finance* 34, no. 1 (2007): 68.
59. Bolch, "Costs Drive Medicaid's Reality," 37.
60. Etienne Pracht, "State Medicaid Managed Care Enrollment: Understanding the Political Calculus that Drives Medicaid Managed Care Reforms," *Journal of Health Politics, Policy & Law* 32, no. 4 (2007): 714.
61. Mark Duggan, "Has the Shift to Managed Care Reduced Medicaid Expenditures? Evidence from State and Local-Level Mandates," *Journal of Policy Analysis and Management* 32.3 (2013): 505–35.
62. Ibid.
63. Anna Aizer, Janet Currie, and Enrico Moretti, "Does Managed Care Hurt Health? Evidence from Medicaid Mothers," *Review of Economics and Statistics* 89, no. 3 (2007): 385–99.
64. Paul Ginsburg, "Achieving Health Care Cost Containment Through Provider Payment Reform That Engages Patients and Providers," *Health Affairs* 32, no. 5 (2013): 931.
65. Fabrice Jotterand, "The Hippocratic Oath and Contemporary Medicine: Dialectic Between Past Ideals and Present Reality?" *Journal of Medicine and Philosophy* 30 (2005): 112.
66. Ibid., 116.
67. Peter Cunningham and Jack Hadley, "Effects of Changes in Incomes and Practice Circumstances on Physicians' Decisions to Treat Charity and Medicaid Patients," *Milbank Quarterly* 86, no. 1 (2008): 94; Ha Tu, "Losing Ground: Physician Income, 1995–2003," *Medical Benefits* 23, no. 17 (2006): 4–5.
68. Sandra Decker, "Medicaid Physician Fees and the Quality of Medical Care of Medicaid Patients in the USA," *Review of Economics of the Household* 5, no. 1 (2007): 98.
69. Ibid., 96.
70. Anna Sommers, Julia Paradise, and Carolyn Miller, "Physician Willingness and Resources to Serve More Medicaid Patients: Perspectives From Primary Care Physicians," *Medicare & Medicaid Research Review* 1, no. 2 (2011): E1–E18.
71. Peter Cunningham and Len Nichols, "The Effects of Medicaid Reimbursement on the Access to Care of Medicaid Enrollees: A Community Perspective," *Med Care Res Rev* 62 (2005): 678.
72. Ibid., 693.
73. B. G. Druss et al., "Comparing the National Economic Burden of Five Chronic Conditions," *Health Affairs* 20, no. 6 (2001): 233–41.
74. Dylan Roby, Gerald Kominski, and Nadereh Pourat, "Assessing the Barriers to

Engaging Challenging Populations in Disease Management Programs: The Medicaid Experience," *Dis Manage Health Outcomes* 16, no. 6 (2008): 421–28.

75. Cunningham and Hadley, "Effects of Changes in Incomes," 91–123.
76. Ibid., 118.
77. Erika Cheng and David A. Kindig, "Disparities in Premature Mortality Between High- and Low-Income US Counties," *Prev Chronic Dis* 9 (2012): 110120; see also Ralph L. Keeney, "Mortality Risks Induced by Economic Expenditures," *Risk Analysis* 10, no. 1 (1990).
78. Diane Rittenhouse, Paula Braveman, and Kristen Marchi, "Improvements in Prenatal Insurance Coverage and Utilization of Care in California: An Unsung Public Health Victory," *Maternal and Child Health Journal* 7, no. 2 (2003): 75–76.
79. US Census Bureau, *Statistical Abstract of the United States 2000* (Washington, DC: US Department of Health and Human Services, 1980).
80. Rittenhouse, Braveman, and Marchi, "Improvements in Prenatal Insurance Coverage," 76.
81. *State Health Watch* (January 2011): 11–12, ISSN 1074-4754.
82. Paula Braveman et al., "Barriers to Timely Prenatal Care among Women with Insurance: The Importance of Prepregnancy Factors," *Obstetrics & Gynecology* 95 (2000): 874.
83. Melissa Nothnagel, Kristen Marchi, Susan Egerter, and Paula Braveman, "Risk Factors for Late or No Prenatal Care Following Medicaid Expansions in California," *Maternal and Child Health Journal* 4, no. 4 (2000): 251–59.
84. Ibid., 256.
85. Ibid., 257.
86. David A. Kindig and Erika R. Cheng, "Even as Mortality Fell in Most US Counties, Female Mortality Nonetheless Rose in 42.8 Percent of Counties from 1992 to 2006," *Health Affairs* 32, no. 3 (2013): 451–58.
87. Ibid., 453–55.
88. Ibid., 455.
89. David Kindig, Paul Peppard, and Bridget Booske, "How Healthy Could a State Be?" *Public Health Reports* 125 (2010): 161.
90. http://www.countyhealthrankings.org/about-project/rankings-background.
91. Steven Woolf and Paula Braveman, "Where Health Disparities Begin: The Role of Social and Economic Determinants—And Why Current Policies May Make Matters Worse," *Health Affairs* 30, no. 10 (2011): 1856.
92. Robert Evans and Gregory Stoddart, "Producing Health, Consuming Health Care," *Soc Sci Med* 31, no. 12 (1990): 1352–53.
93. Peter Muening et al., "The Relative Health Burden of Selected Social and Behavioral Risk Factors in the United States: Implications for Policy," *Am J Public Health* 100, no. 9 (2010): 1762.
94. Ibid.
95. Woolf and Braveman, "Where Health Disparities Begin," 1853.
96. Gable, "The Patient Protection and Affordable Care Act," 341.
97. Ibid., 346.

PART 4:

MEDICAID'S HEALTH CARE FAILURES AND POSSIBLE REFORMS

CHAPTER 7: REFORMING MEDICAID

JAMES C. CAPRETTA

The Medicaid program today bears little resemblance to the program Congress thought it was creating nearly a half century ago. The priority for the drafters of the 1965 amendments to the Social Security Act was creating health insurance for the elderly—Medicare. Medicaid received far less attention.[1] The drafters thought they were providing federal structure and uniformity, as well as some funding, for the many state programs long in existence that were already providing "indigent care." The congressional authors of the legislation were not aware that what they were setting in motion was a program that would become the largest entitlement—by enrollment—in the United States. Today, Medicaid costs federal and state taxpayers $440 billion annually and serves about 70 million people.[2]

Medicaid's financing and programmatic problems are rooted in its original legislative design. As a shared federal–state program, it is financed partly by the federal government and partly by the state, resulting in split political accountability. State officials often blame the federal government for imposing costly mandates in Medicaid, even as federal officials and agencies increasingly blame the states for using the program as a means of tapping federal taxpayers to solve their budgetary problems.

The method by which Medicaid's costs are assigned to the federal and state governments—a state-specific federal match rate—is a primary source of the program's perverse incentives. On average, the federal matching rate is 57 percent of state Medicaid costs, meaning the federal government covers $0.57 of every $1.00 in state-initiated Medicaid spending. Because there is no upper limit on federal Medicaid funding, states can reduce their budgetary costs if they are able to move programs traditionally financed with state-only funds under the Medicaid programmatic umbrella, thus drawing partial federal support. Not surprisingly, this has been a common practice among the states for many years.[3] (For more on states' budgetary incentives, see chapters 1 and 4, pages 9 and 65.)

Further, the Medicaid matching formula undermines the incentive for spending discipline at the state level. The shared financing of Medicaid means that states can initiate new spending in Medicaid and have it partially financed by federal taxpayers; but the flip side is that state-initiated Medicaid spending cuts must also be shared with federal taxpayers. So, for instance, in a state where the federal government is financing 60 percent of Medicaid spending, the governor and state legislators face the unattractive prospect of keeping only $1 in savings for every $2.50 in Medicaid spending cuts they can identify and implement. The other $1.50 in savings is returned to the federal treasury. This kind of formula is a major disincentive to cost-cutting by state politicians.

Widespread recognition of these and other shortcomings in Medicaid have led to near continuous calls to reform the program, both at the federal and state levels of government. To date, these reform efforts have not yielded fundamental transformation of the program.

THE WAIVER OPTION

Medicaid rests on an uneasy federal–state relationship. The federal government finances more than half of the program, but the states initiate the spending. Not surprisingly, because federal taxpayers are on the hook for a substantial (and unlimited) portion of the costs, the federal government has not hesitated to steadily impose more and more federal controls over the program's basic operations, through legislative as well as regulatory changes. These changes have mainly come in the form of new "mandates"—requirements that compel states to operate their Medicaid programs in conformance with an ever-expanding list of federal rules. These mandates affect everything from what states must provide in terms of covered services, to minimum payments to providers, to the categories of beneficiaries that must be made eligible for Medicaid coverage. For instance, from the beginning, the Medicaid statute required certain kinds of preventive services be provided to eligible children, but the definition of what is required was substantially broadened in legislation enacted in 1989.[4] Every state must conform to that one national rule.

The impulse for the growing federal role in the program is, of course, rooted in part in the expectation that whoever is paying the bills (or the biggest part of them) should have a say in how the money is spent. But probably even more important has been the straightforward impulse to expand benefits and services to low-income populations. That has been a motivation for politicians in both parties.

For their part, the states have often resisted the proposals for new mandates and required coverage expansions considered by Congress and the Department of Health and Human Services (HHS)—but many expansions have occurred nonetheless.[5] The desire to expand Medicaid's reach to more and more people, and to cover more and more services, has proven to be far more powerful than any hesitancy about violating the terms of the original understanding of Medicaid, which was that the federal government would provide the overall structure for the program, but the states would have the biggest say in who is entitled and to what benefits.

The tension that the steady increase of federal control over Medicaid has created in the relationship with the states has manifested itself in several ways, but most especially in the rapid increase in state-initiated waiver requests.

The Social Security Act comprises the set of laws that addresses the Social Security program as well as Medicare and Medicaid. In Section 1115 of that act, Congress delegated to HHS the authority to waive certain requirements under the act in order to allow demonstrations of new approaches to implementing social welfare programs, including Medicaid. In addition, the Medicaid law itself includes waiver authority, allowing states to apply to HHS to utilize more managed care approaches to delivering Medicaid services (and thus exclude some doctors and hospitals from the Medicaid network of providers). States can also seek waivers to use Medicaid funds to pay for home- and community-based long-term care services instead of only using Medicaid to pay for nursing home care.

The use of waivers to run state Medicaid programs has become widespread. Indeed, anytime a state decides to pursue large-scale changes to how they run Medicaid, it is the norm, not the exception, to embed those changes in the context of a waiver request to the federal government. According to the database that HHS has made available online, 381 current waiver programs of all types have been approved by HHS and are in operation in the states, of which 41 are existing Section 1115 waivers.[6] Section 1115 waivers give the secretary of HHS the authority to initiate "experimental, pilot, or demonstration projects that promote the objectives of the Medicaid and CHIP programs. The purpose of these demonstrations, which give States additional flexibility to design and improve their programs, is to demonstrate and evaluate policy approaches."[7] Approximately 24 waiver requests are now pending at HHS.[8]

The statute intends that the federal government and the states will use waivers to test new concepts for a period of years, followed by an evaluation. If a test falls short of expectations, the waiver would be expected to be discontinued. Similarly, successes would presumably influence national policy making for the other states.

The reality is very different. States have used waivers not so much to test new ideas, but to manage their programs outside of the constraints of some statutory provisions. In some notable cases, states have used Section 1115 waivers to pursue changes that constitute fundamental reform of how Medicaid operates or how Medicaid fits into the broader health system. Three state-initiated waivers from the past several years are noteworthy in this regard and provide good examples of the creative use of the Section 1115 waiver authority.

Indiana requested a waiver to allow persons just above the normal Medicaid income eligibility levels to enroll in a special insurance program featuring the use of health savings account (HSA)-style spending arrangement. The idea was to give these mainly uninsured residents of the state an insurance plan with out-of-pocket financial protection, and also a personally owned spending account to cover the cost of services below the relatively high (for Medicaid) insurance deductible. Indiana's governor at the time, Republican Mitch Daniels, pushed for the waiver on the grounds that it would expand coverage to many thousands of the uninsured in the state by using an approach that would promote consumer-directed health care and cost-conscious consumption of services.[9] Medicaid funding was used both to subsidize the higher deductible insurance and to place funds in the HSA accounts for use by the enrollees. Indiana's original waiver was approved in 2007.

By all accounts, the Indiana experiment in HSAs worked very well for state residents. Enrollment exceeded 45,000 in just the first two years of the program, and the cost and health experience were very positive.[10] According to an evaluation conducted by Mathematica Policy Research, the low-income participants in the Indiana initiative found the HSA approach attractive, with large percentages making contributions to their accounts to build assets for future health needs. Nonetheless, Indiana has been forced to engage in a protracted negotiation with HHS to get the waiver extended. In early September

2013, the Centers for Medicare and Medicaid Services (CMS) finally granted a one-year extension for the Indiana Medicaid waiver program.[11] And yet, despite the one-year reprieve, the long-term future for the program remains very much uncertain.

In Rhode Island in 2009, then-governor Donald Carcieri, a Republican, proposed to fundamentally transform the Medicaid program in the state by converting the federal contribution to the state program into a global cap on the program. Many viewed this proposal as a state-initiated version of a federal block grant. Instead of paying for a fixed percentage of Rhode Island's Medicaid costs, Governor Carcieri proposed that the federal government provide to the state a fixed total amount of federal funding regardless of the state's spending experience. In return for giving the federal government budgetary certainty, the state asked for substantial new flexibility to manage the benefits and populations covered by the program without regard to many federal rules. The administration of President George W. Bush approved the waiver in early 2009.

The Rhode Island waiver provoked strong negative reaction from those who thought it gave Rhode Island too much authority to unilaterally manage the program.[12] Supporters championed the proposal as a test of the Medicaid block grant concept. Early evaluations of the program showed that it largely met the expectations of Rhode Island officials. According to an independent assessment, the flexibility Rhode Island gained under the waiver allowed the state to generate "significant savings," including $36 million over three years in reduced nursing home costs.[13]

In Massachusetts, an entirely different approach to reform was pursued by then-governor Mitt Romney in 2006. He proposed a waiver that would allow the state of Massachusetts to move federal funding for what are known as disproportionate share hospitals (DSH) into a new subsidized insurance scheme for persons not eligible for Medicaid. It was well known at the time that Massachusetts was in danger of losing the federal DSH funding entirely because of the illegitimate mechanism used to pay for the state's portion of the cost. To prevent the loss of funding, Governor Romney, a Republican, worked with the state's Democratic legislature to propose a waiver that eventually became the model for President Obama's national reform legislation. In addition to moving the federal DSH funding into an insurance subsidy program, Massachusetts enacted an individual mandate on state residents, thus requiring everyone in the state to secure government-approved health coverage. It also created the "Connector" through which some state residents would use their new state subsidy for health insurance to purchase coverage from among competing private insurance plans.

The Massachusetts Medicaid waiver of 2006 was the most consequential waiver ever approved by the federal government. The Obama administration has argued forcefully that its adoption—on a bipartisan basis—by Massachusetts state politicians should have led Republicans at the national level to embrace the Patient Protection and Affordable Care Act (ACA),[14] which shared some common elements with the Massachusetts program. But many in the GOP countered that the national law has given far more sweeping powers to the federal government than were handed to the Massachusetts state government under the 2006 waiver. Moreover, it is a very different matter to enact a state program from which other states can differ than to enact one national program that all states must adopt. Even so, it is undeniable that the approval of the Massachusetts waiver was an important step along the way to enactment of the sweeping national legislation.[15]

BUDGET NEUTRALITY AND THE WAIVER NEGOTIATION PROCESS

The federal government has approved scores of waiver requests for the states over the past four decades, but some have not been approved and more still have only been approved after a lengthy and oftentimes contentious negotiation between federal and state officials over the content of the waiver request.[16]

To some extent, ideology has played a role in the attitude of various administrations toward state Medicaid waiver requests. Republican administrations have tended to look favorably on requests to use more private insurance options to cover the Medicaid population. Democratic administrations have favored approaches that bring into Medicaid larger numbers of low-income residents.

But by far the most important consideration in any significant waiver request is the money. More specifically, the waiver requests from the states are assessed to determine whether or not they are budget neutral, meaning they are assessed to determine whether the federal government would pay more to the state under the waiver than it would without the waiver. Not surprisingly, this is the source of frequent disagreements between the states and the federal government.

The concept of budget neutrality in Medicaid waiver assessments dates back to the early 1980s. Prior to that time, HHS could approve state Medicaid requests under Section 1115 of the Social Security Act without regard to the waivers' impact on federal spending. The statute never mentions budget neutrality as a requirement for federal approval of the demonstration programs.

As HHS approved more and more requests by the states to waive certain Medicaid statutory provisions, the White House Office of Management and Budget (OMB) became concerned that the state programs being approved by HHS were actually costing the federal government substantially more than the regular Medicaid program. In 1983, early in the Reagan administration, OMB and HHS came to an agreement that all future Section 1115 waivers must be budget neutral to the federal government over the life of the demonstration.[17] This agreement also gave OMB the authority to reject demonstration requests from the states that did not meet the test of neutrality. Since that time, OMB has played a central role in virtually all federal–state negotiations over significant waiver requests.

The budget neutrality test implies that the administration can apply an objective measure of financial rigor to assess the merits of state waiver requests. Unfortunately, the reality is that assessing budget neutrality entails far more subjective judgments than any of the participants would care to admit.

The problem begins with the fact that the federal government does not maintain a 50-state baseline of Medicaid costs.[18] The actuaries employed by CMS create a federal Medicaid baseline at least twice a year, with projections going out 10 years. But that baseline reflects aggregate federal Medicaid expenditures, not state-by-state spending. So, when a significant waiver request is made by a state, the actuaries have to construct a special state-only baseline estimate.

There are no definitive rules for doing this. For instance, what is the future growth rate of Medicaid expenditures in a given state? Is it the same as the assumed national trend rate? What if the state has had slower growth in recent years, or a changing demographic profile? Should that be factored into the assessment? And what about state claims that the waiver program will operate more efficiently than the existing program, or improve the health status of the served population and thus lower future costs? Is there validity to those claims? These are the typical questions at the heart of the federal–state negotiations over waivers.

And when there is so much room for judgment involved in assessing what is or is not budget neutral, the decision to approve or disapprove a waiver is inevitably moved from the civil service level to the political level. Thus, the boundaries of objective budgetary assessment are moved into the realm of more ambiguous political negotiation. With so much money at stake, states become heavily invested in the process. They lobby HHS and the White House vigorously; they make calls to the president's political advisors; Congressional delegations become involved. The result is that the waiver approval process is a high-stakes political affair that has the feel of a legislative negotiation rather than consideration based on objective measures of a temporary test of a new idea, as the statute warrants.

It follows, too, that this kind of process leads to strong suspicions that the politically connected get the best deals. States with strong political connections to the White House are assumed to receive more favorable judgments on how to calculate the state-specific Medicaid spending baseline, and thus provide more funding to those states under their waiver requests. This widespread perception of favoritism only further incents states to treat the entire endeavor as a highly politicized process, which means hiring a team of expensive lobbyists and using pressure from elected lawmakers from the state to pressure the administration to grant the waiver request.

The subjectivity of the Medicaid waiver approval process raises questions of fundamental fairness. Why should taxpayers in one state receive more favorable treatment than those in another state based on an idiosyncratic waiver approval process?

For this and other reasons, a better approach to fundamental Medicaid reform can be found in proposals to remake the program through federal legislation.

STATUTORY REFORM OPTIONS AT THE FEDERAL LEVEL

An effective Medicaid reform at the federal level would, first and foremost, address the fundamental flaw in Medicaid's current design: the matching formula used to establish the federal–state split on Medicaid costs. As stated previously, this approach to financing Medicaid undermines spending discipline and causes budgetary problems for the federal government as well as the states.

One approach to reform would be to convert the federal contribution to the states into a fixed federal block grant that would not be altered based on additional state spending. The idea would be to provide budgetary certainty to the federal government and the states and to provide strong incentives to the states to manage the federal funding prudently. Under a block grant, cost overruns at the state level would be financed entirely by state taxpayers, not the federal government. Conversely, the federal contribution to a state would not decrease if the state found ways to cut Medicaid costs. All of the savings from rooting out waste and efficiency would accrue to state taxpayers. This is how the state children's health insurance program has been structured since enactment in 1997.

The key issue in converting to a block grant is establishing the basis by which the federal government will make payments to the states. One option would be to examine historical Medicaid spending levels by the federal government in the various states over a preceding number of years, such as perhaps the three most recent years. The first year of the block grant could then be calculated as the average of federal Medicaid spending in the state per year during that period of time, inflated to the year in question by the national Medicaid spending growth rate.

Once the first year is settled, the question becomes how to inflate the federal Medicaid block grant amounts in future years. The indexing options include using the consumer price index (CPI), which historically is well below medical inflation, the growth rate of the national economy as measured by gross domestic product (GDP), or perhaps a measure of national or regional health spending growth. The decision on indexing is highly consequential because alternative approaches can result in large differences in federal spending over time. If the block grant is pursued in part to help ease the nation's severe, long-term budgetary challenges, then indexing the block grant amounts to something below the historical rate of growth for Medicaid can produce significant savings estimates, especially over the long term.

The budget resolution that passed the US House of Representatives in March 2013 assumed Medicaid was converted to a block grant and indexed to the CPI plus population growth in the states—a rate well below the historical rate of Medicaid spending inflation and well below what the Congressional Budget Office (CBO) assumes will occur absent a change in the legislation. Consequently, the House-passed budget's Medicaid plan would substantially reduce federal costs over the coming decade.[19]

Using historical rates of spending to establish the initial state block grant amounts locks into the block grant whatever irrational disparities in federal support exist today among the states. Some proposals try to correct for large gaps between states by indexing the block grant amounts at differential rates. For instance, low-cost states might be indexed at a slightly higher-than-average rate, whereas high-cost states could be indexed at a rate below the national average. Proposals that make these kinds of adjustments necessarily generate a great deal of attention from the states and their representatives in Congress. The danger is that attempting to redistribute Medicaid funding among the states while also reforming the program could create so much political opposition that the reform fails. Consequently, reformers may instead want to enact a reform first that changes the nature of the federal–state financial relationship based on historical patterns of federal spending per state before addressing approaches to narrowing gaps among the states.

Opponents of the block grant concept argue that it will necessarily result in a reduction in services for vulnerable populations. But that is far from certain; the current program, with open-ended federal matching payments, provides strong incentives to the states to move as much spending as possible under the Medicaid umbrella, and little incentive to carefully scrutinize expenditures. With a block grant, the states would have strong incentives to eliminate waste without undermining coverage for those who truly need it.

In 1996, similar arguments were made about the block granting of welfare funding, with predictions that it would lead to significant hardship for the program's enrollees. What happened instead is that the states reviewed who was on the cash assistance program and quickly found that many of them were capable of entering the workforce and improving their household incomes from wages instead of government assistance. By 2000, the cash welfare rolls had fallen by about half even as the population in the bottom fifth of the income distribution experienced substantial gains in their real incomes.[20]

Health coverage is more complicated than cash welfare, but there is every reason to expect that substantial inefficiency exists in Medicaid, and that a block grant would provide the incentive to find and eliminate it.

Still, concerns about the effect that a block grant might have on health services for the vulnerable has led to proposals that mitigate against some of the financial risks a block grant would entail. The most prominent example of such a proposal is per capita caps.

Under per capita caps, the federal government would establish for each state a per person payment based on the main eligibility categories in the Medicaid program: the elderly, the blind and disabled, nondisabled adults, and children. The federal government would then make payments to the states based on the number of Medicaid enrollees in each of these categories. The per capita payment would be based on historical spending rates for the various categories of beneficiaries in each state, and, again, would be indexed to a predetermined growth rate.[21]

Per capita caps in Medicaid would have the same advantages as a block grant in that the states would have strong incentives to use the federal funding wisely. The amount of the federal payment per person would be the same regardless of how much the state spent on each enrollee. The only difference with the block grant is that the states would not be at risk for increased enrollment in the program because the per capita payments would be made for all enrollees in the program, including those who might not have been expected to sign up and thus were excluded from the block grant formula. This could be important in times of slow economic growth or during a recession, when Medicaid enrollment typically surges.

Perhaps most important, per capita caps have enjoyed bipartisan support in the past. In 1995 and 1996, the Clinton administration proposed Medicaid per capita caps as part of a larger balanced budget plan. That proposal was explicitly endorsed by 46 Senate Democrats in a letter to the president in December 1995.[22]

Both the block grant and per capita caps would remove from the program the distorted incentives that flow from today's matching rate approach to Medicaid financing. They would also free up the states to pursue reforms that, until now, have been difficult to implement in Medicaid because of federal concerns. Specifically, states that would like to pursue more market-driven Medicaid reform could move directly to convert the program from what might be called a "defined benefit" model of insurance to one based on defined contributions. Instead of entitling beneficiaries to a set of services, states could give Medicaid participants a fixed level of support—a defined-contribution payment—and then allow the Medicaid beneficiaries to use that support to pick from among a number of competing insurance options. The Indiana approach of using the defined contributions to fund an HSA-like account could be part of the reform.

This approach to state-driven Medicaid reform would use competition and consumer choice to hold down costs instead of the unrealistically low payment rates that are now used by states to cut payments to doctors and hospitals. Nonelderly and disabled beneficiaries would be free to choose from among competing insurance options, which would create pressure on the insurance plans to provide better access to care than is provided under today's Medicaid program. Under this approach, states would need to ensure the defined contribution was adequate to get reliable insurance, but it would also create pressure to hold down costs because the Medicaid participants could keep the savings from enrolling in lower-premium plans.

States could also pursue a defined-contribution approach for their elderly and disabled populations The purpose would not be to finance insurance enrollment but to provide resources for the direct purchase of needed long-term support services. One approach would be to establish a maximum contribution based on a severely disabled person needing extensive support. Persons with lesser disabilities would get a fraction of the maximum amount commensurate with their needs. The recipients, and their families and caregivers, would then use the fixed level of support from Medicaid to secure services from a competing list of approved service providers. This approach would foster strong price competition and allow the recipients and their families to target their resources on their most significant needs.[23]

A main objective of this type of reform for the elderly and disabled would be to reduce the use of expensive nursing home care by improving the services available for those who remain in the community. However, some state residents will still require nursing home assistance. The cost of nursing home care could be provided outside of the defined-contribution context, with the state paying directly for those services, perhaps on contracts awarded to nursing homes with the higher-quality indicators and reasonable costs.

A federal move toward block grants or per capita caps would provide much greater budgetary control at the federal level. States could achieve a similar level of enhanced budgetary control by moving to a defined-contribution approach. Instead of unpredictable and open-ended benefit commitments, a state could provide fixed levels of support to program participants. Opponents will say this is an unfair shift of risk onto the program's participants. But a shift to defined-contribution payments would not result in reduced benefits if it brings about new levels of efficiency and productivity in the provision of services. Indeed, the whole point of such a reform is to foster competition and innovation that improve the quality of choices for the program's enrollees, not worsen them. And there is strong evidence from other market-driven models, like the Medicare drug benefit, that competition and choice will have exactly this effect on costs in Medicaid.[24]

CONCLUSION

The Medicaid program is now a dominant part of American health care, but there has always been uneasiness about its design, dating all the way back to its enactment in 1965. Costs have grown so much that they threaten to push federal and state budgets past the breaking point. Although millions of Americans rely on Medicaid, there is much evidence that the program falls well short of the quality care that the population deserves.

The fundamental problem in Medicaid is that neither the federal government nor the states are fully in charge. Those who favor more centralized control over the nation's health system would like to resolve the tension in Medicaid by federalizing more and more aspects of the program. That is why the health care law passed in 2010 required 100 percent federal funding for the first three years of the anticipated expansion. However, to date, less than half of the states have adopted the expansion, despite the promise of full, but temporary, federal financing. Based on the program's long history, many state governors and legislators are wary of setting in motion another long-term spending commitment within Medicaid that could burden future state taxpayers. Many state governors are also generally opposed to the 2010 health care law and would prefer to replace it with an approach that would elicit more bipartisan support.

Some states have pushed back against the steady federalization of Medicaid by pursuing various waiver approaches. But these waiver plans must still be approved by the federal government, which can be a large political exercise as well as a budget exercise, leaving states in the position of investing time and resources into securing Washington's approval of their plans.

A more permanent and stable approach to reform would fundamentally transform the nature of the federal–state relationship. Instead of micromanaging Medicaid, the federal government could provide a fixed level of support through Medicaid, with the states deciding how to spend those federal funds, as well as state resources, to help their low-income populations secure the health services they need. This kind of transformation of Medicaid could come with strong accountability provisions for the states, including measures of the health status of their vulnerable populations as well as estimates of insurance coverage rates. States would then have the freedom to manage the programs to improve the lives of their citizens, and could be held accountable by state voters.

NOTES

1. Judith G. Moore and David G. Smith, "Legislating Medicaid: Considering Medicaid and Its Origins," *Health Care Financing Review* 27, no. 2 (Winter 2005–2006), http://www.cms.gov/Research-Statistics-Data-and-Systems/Research/HealthCareFinancingReview/downloads/05-06Winpg45.pdf.
2. Congressional Budget Office, "Medicaid Spending and Enrollment Detail for CBO's

May 2013 Medicaid Baseline," May 2013, http://www.cbo.gov/sites/default/files/cbofiles/attachments/44204_Medicaid.pdf.

3. For instance, in 2010, the state of Connecticut moved a state-funded and capped health insurance assistance program for low-income adults without children under Medicaid in order to secure federal matching funds. Ironically, the governor at the time, M. Jodi Rell, argued against the shift on the basis that it would be more difficult to control enrollment once the program became part of a broader Medicaid entitlement. See Keith M. Phaneuf, "Bill Cuts Most of This Year's Deficit," *Connecticut Mirror*, April 15, 2010, http://www.ctmirror.com/story/2010/04/14/bill-cuts-most-years-deficit. Between 2010 and 2013, enrollment in the program grew from 45,000 to 86,000. See Keith M. Phaneuf, "Malloy Takes to Air to Rebut Budget Critics," *Connecticut Mirror*, May 6, 2013, http://www.ctmirror.org/story/2013/05/06/malloy-takes-air-rebut-budget-critics.

4. Commonwealth Fund, "EPSDT: An Overview," September 2005, http://www.commonwealthfund.org/~/media/Files/Publications/Data%20Brief/2005/Sep/EPSDT%20%20An%20Overview/893_EPSDT_overview%20pdf.pdf.

5. See table 2 of Jonathan Gruber, "Medicaid" (Working Paper 7829, National Bureau of Economic Research, Cambridge, MA, August 2000), http://www.nber.org/papers/w7829.pdf, for a list of the many incremental legislative expansions of the program from 1965 to 2000.

6. The HHS waiver database is available at http://www.medicaid.gov/Medicaid-CHIP-Program-Information/By-Topics/Waivers/Waivers.html.

7. http://www.medicaid.gov/Medicaid-CHIP-Program-Information/By-Topics/Waivers/1115/Section-1115-Demonstrations.html.

8. As of July 2013. For a current list of pending waivers, see http://www.medicaid.gov/Medicaid-CHIP-Program-Information/By-Topics/Waivers/1115/Pending-1115-Demonstration-Applications-.html.

9. See the waiver request letter from Governor Mitchell E. Daniels Jr. to Secretary Michael O. Leavitt, February 28, 2007, http://svcinc.org/PDF/Waiver22807.pdf.

10. Timothy K. Lake, Vivian L. H. Byrd, and Seema Verma, "Healthy Indiana Plan: Lessons for Reform" (Issue Brief No. 1, Mathematic Policy Research, Inc., Princeton, NJ, January 2011), http://www.mathematica-mpr.com/publications/PDFs/health/healthyindianaplan_ib1.pdf.

11. Family and Social Services Administration, State of Indiana, "Background, on the Healthy Indiana Plan Waiver," FSSA Backgrounder, September 3, 2013, http://www.in.gov/fssa/hip/files/BACKGROUND_ON_THE_HEALTHY_INDIANA_PLAN_WAIVER.pdf.

12. Jesse Cross-Call and Judith Solomon, "Rhode Island's Global Waiver Not a Model for How States Would Fare under a Medicaid Block Grant" (Washington, DC: Center on Budget and Policy Priorities, March 2011), http://www.cbpp.org/files/3-16-11health2.pdf.

13. The Lewin Group, *An Independent Evaluation of Rhode Island's Global Waiver*, December 2011, http://www.ohhs.ri.gov/documents/documents11/Lewin_report_12_6_11.pdf.

14. Patient Protection and Affordable Care Act, Pub. L. No. 111-148, 124 Stat. 119 (2010) (codified as amended sections of 42 U.S.C.).

15. Jonathan Gruber, a key advisor to both the Massachusetts and national reform efforts, has repeatedly made the argument that the Massachusetts plan paved the way for the national program, and that if Massachusetts had not gone first, the national effort, in all likelihood, would not have succeeded. See "Romney Defends Mass. Health Care

Law," *Boston Globe*, March 30, 2010, http://www.boston.com/news/health/articles/2010/03/30/romney_defends_massachusetts_health_care_law/?page=full. Governor Mitt Romney maintained in the 2012 presidential campaign that the Massachusetts plan was suited only to Massachusetts and would not work nationally. See Avik Roy, "Romney's Revenge: Romney said His Bay State Health Reforms Weren't Necessarily Suited to Other States. Few Listened," *National Review Online*, June 18, 2013, http://www.nationalreview.com/article/351197/romneys-revenge-avik-roy.

16. Denials of Medicaid waiver requests are often not the end of the story. States frequently ask permission to make changes in their Medicaid program, are denied, and then come back to HHS with an amended request that might meet approval. This process gives HHS a great deal of power to steer states away from policies that are viewed unfavorably by the federal bureaucracy without issuing a full disapproval of an entire waiver request. See, for instance, Michelle Oxman, "Why CMS Refused Florida Medicaid 'Reform' Waiver," *Law and Health Blog*, Wolters Kluwer, February 21, 2012, http://health.wolterskluwerlb.com/2012/02/why-cms-refused-florida-medicaid-reform-waiver/.

17. Cynthia Shirk, "Shaping Medicaid and SCHIP Through Waivers: The Fundamentals" (Background Paper No. 64, National Health Policy Forum, Washington, DC, July 2008), http://www.nhpf.org/library/background-papers/BP64_MedicaidSCHIP.Waivers_07-22-08.pdf.

18. A baseline is a budget projection based on current law and current policy. The concept is intended to create a set of figures from which alternative policies, including law changes, can be measured. For a longer discussion of the concept of budget baselines, see Timothy J. Muris, "The Uses and Abuses of Budget Baselines," in *The Budget Puzzle: Understanding Federal Spending*, John F. Cogan, Timothy J. Muris, and Allen Schick (Stanford, CA: Stanford University Press, 1994).

19. House Budget Committee, "The Path to Prosperity: A Responsible Balanced Budget," March 2013, http://budget.house.gov/uploadedfiles/fy14budget.pdf.

20. See Pamela J. Loprest, "How Has the TANF Caseload Changed Over Time" (Brief 8, Urban Institute Washington, DC, March 2012), http://www.acf.hhs.gov/sites/default/files/opre/change_time_1.pdf; and Congressional Budget Office, "Changes in the Economic Resources of Households with Low-Income Children," May 2007, http://www.cbo.gov/sites/default/files/cbofiles/ftpdocs/81xx/doc8113/05-16-low-income.pdf.

21. Fred Upton and Orrin Hatch, "Making Medicaid Work: Protect the Vulnerable, Offer Individualized Care, and Reduce Costs," May 2013, http://energycommerce.house.gov/sites/republicans.energycommerce.house.gov/files/analysis/20130501Medicaid.pdf.

22. See Cong. Rec. 19185, vol. 141, no. 207 (December 22, 1995), http://www.gpo.gov/fdsys/pkg/CREC-1995-12-22/pdf/CREC-1995-12-22-pt1-PgS19185.pdf.

23. For a more detailed description of this concept, see James C. Capretta et al., "Assuring a Future for Long-Term Care Services and Supports in Texas" (Austin, TX: Texas Public Policy Foundation, December 2012), http://www.texaspolicy.com/sites/default/files/documents/2012-12-RR09-AssuringFutureLongTermCareServices-CHCP-Capretta.pdf.

24. For a discussion of the success of the Medicare drug benefit, see James C. Capretta, "Congress Should Not Undermine What Works in the Medicare Drug Benefit" (Web Memo 3360, Heritage Foundation, Washington, DC, September 9, 2011), http://www.heritage.org/research/reports/2011/09/medicare-drug-benefit-model-for-broader-healthcare-reform.

CHAPTER 8: HOW TO ACHIEVE SUSTAINABLE MEDICAID REFORM

THOMAS P. MILLER

The Patient Protection and Affordable Care Act (ACA)[1] could put as many as 16 million to 17 million more low-income Americans into Medicaid (and the related Children's Health Insurance Program (CHIP)) coverage over the next decade, but without making significant structural changes in how the Medicaid program operates.[2] Although those initial coverage estimates, made in 2010, have been revised downward in light of a Supreme Court decision in June 2012 that essentially made the Medicaid expansion a state option,[3] additional enrollment in Medicaid remains a key part of insurance coverage expansion plans under the ACA, which begin primarily in 2014.

Even before this latest effort to expand the program for low-income Americans is implemented, Medicaid was already nearing a fiscal and operational crisis. State budgets were buckling under the weight of their share of Medicaid program costs. Medicaid spending increasingly "crowded" out other important areas of state spending, such as education and investments in rebuilding local infrastructure. The networks of physicians and hospitals willing to see large numbers of Medicaid patients continued to shrink, and the quality of care provided to Medicaid enrollees was quite disappointing, to say the least.[4] Medicaid's low rates of reimbursement for health care providers also led to efforts to shift at least some of those extra costs to private health insurance premiums.[5] At the same time, the Medicaid program remained a fertile ground for fraudulent claims for reimbursement.[6]

Medicaid's spending incentives often operate at cross purposes in stimulating demand while restricting supply. Its open-ended "match rate" incentives for federal financial support (the federal medical assistance percentage, or FMAP), in which each dollar of state Medicaid spending is matched by at least one dollar (or more) from federal taxpayers, discourage state efforts to control such spending. Medicaid's comprehensive list of covered benefits, with minimal cost-sharing by beneficiaries, further adds to increased use of health care services.

On the other hand, even states benefiting from matching federal funds and creative ways to maximize them beyond their nominal percentage levels can run up against their own budget limits when dealing with periods of economic downturn and managing competing claims on their resources. Their most common policy response has been to lower payments to Medicaid providers, even further below their actual costs to supply covered services and products.[7] Cutbacks in optional Medicaid benefits and limits on eligibility offer less immediate savings to state policy makers. They also are more transparent to voters and Medicaid beneficiaries, and hence less politically attractive. More recently, the ACA's new requirements for "maintenance of effort" within state Medicaid programs have further limited short-term economizing options, mostly to reductions in provider reimbursement rates.

The overall effect of this push–pull dynamic in Medicaid's conflicting financial incentives is to increase demands on a program that is already struggling to do more with less, and failing at both tasks. The inevitable result of hollow benefit promises to more beneficiaries that try to be delivered below their actual costs is less value per taxpayer dollar.

The distortions in today's open-ended Medicaid matching program for federal financial support that encourage higher overall costs will be magnified as the ACA temporarily increases the federal match for all states to 100 percent for the population of new program participants, beginning in 2014. (The pre-ACA average matching rate for the federal share of total Medicaid spending nationally was 57 percent.) Some, if not all, participating states will respond to this incentive by reducing their efforts to control Medicaid's costs for newly eligible enrollees and by looking for ways to move more costs from their books and onto the federal budget while they can.[8]

The perverse incentives within Medicaid's structure extend far beyond their adverse impact on government budgets and health care reimbursement. Medicaid was originally established in 1965 to provide health coverage to welfare recipients. Most states established automatic "categorical" eligibility for Medicaid to their residents who also were enrolled in other federal programs that legally entitled them to welfare assistance (primarily under the Aid to Families with Dependent Children program, before that program's eligibility rules were revised extensively in the mid-1990s and mostly "delinked" from Medicaid eligibility). Over the years, Medicaid has moved away from that approach, with more eligibility for coverage based strictly on income tests that may vary by state. But even today, Medicaid is not integrated into the insurance system for working-age Americans. It stands apart as a separate structure, with no coordination or transition between Medicaid coverage and private health insurance.

This lack of coordination between the two spheres of insurance for lower-income Americans causes serious problems for Medicaid beneficiaries. When they earn more, they often lose eligibility for Medicaid, even if they face uncertain insurance prospects in the employer-based market. This continues to create employment disincentives. Movement back and forth between Medicaid and private insurance plans can also disrupt ongoing relationships with physicians who are in private insurance networks but not part of a state's Medicaid plan.

REPEAL AND RESISTANCE, WITHOUT REFORM, IS NOT SUFFICIENT

Even though all of these chronic problems plaguing Medicaid will only be amplified under the ACA, critics of the law need to do more than urge simple repeal of its Medicaid provisions or resistance by state governments to expansion of their Medicaid coverage. Moving a modernized Medicaid program beyond its mistakes of the pre-ACA past will require sustainable, substantive reforms.

The lower bounds of necessary reform begin, but do not end, with setting realistic limits on taxpayers' commitments to finance necessary health care services for low-income Americans. Finding a new sustainable balance between Medicaid's levels of eligibility, covered benefits, provider reimbursement, and beneficiary choice requires more flexible tradeoffs, better targeting, decentralized decision making, and more transparent accountability to both taxpayers and enrollees.

The upper bounds of Medicaid reform suggest that the program would perform better by promising less and concentrating more on its core mission of ensuring improved health care outcomes for those most in need. This will entail less emphasis on the quantity of health services it provides and more on their quality. Improving the effectiveness of Medicaid in the lives of low-income Americans will also entail bolstering other areas of public policy that shape the magnitude and nature of the demand for its assistance, as well as the likelihood of the program's success.

TESTING THE LOWER AND UPPER BOUNDS OF A MEDICAID REFORM AGENDA

How do we adjust a Medicaid reform agenda to ensure not only that the necessary lower bounds are attained, but that progress toward the upper bounds is not sacrificed? A more realistic look at the necessary public policy changes falls into four broad categories:

- Structuring sustainable fiscal limits and incentives
- Improving health care delivery

- Developing a compelling political rationale
- Facilitating opportunities for innovation

This chapter will focus primarily on the first category of policy changes, with some additional thoughts on the other ones that will help strengthen and sustain them.

FISCAL REFORM

First, the challenge of publicly financing Medicaid should be placed in perspective. Since its initial enactment in 1965, Medicaid's annual rates of spending growth have varied substantially—in part because of different trends in the annual rate of enrollment growth versus the program's annual growth rate for spending per enrollee. An important factor involves the changing composition of Medicaid enrollees (the relative rates of enrollment growth for higher-cost and lower-cost beneficiaries, such as the disabled versus younger mothers and their children). It has been partly driven by policy changes involving eligibility (for example, newly covered populations in the 1990s, and others arriving into the program's coverage under the ACA next year) and categories of covered benefits (for example, moving prescription drug coverage in 2006 to Medicare for dual eligible seniors).

The long-term historical trend has been for Medicaid expenditures per enrollee to grow at a slower rate than overall national health spending per capita. For Medicaid, the average annual rate was 7.7 percent from 1971 through 2010 (note that all of the following years used in this section represent fiscal years, rather than calendar years). The average annual growth rate for national per capita health spending during that period was 8.2 percent. However, Medicaid enrollment growth over those four decades also averaged 3.4 percent per year, boosting overall average annual growth in Medicaid spending to 11.4 percent.[9]

The difference in average annual growth rates has been much larger recently, with Medicaid spending per enrollee growing by 2.5 percent per year and overall national health spending per capita by 5.6 percent per year from 2001 through 2010.[10]

Medicaid spending growth trends varied even more at different times within this period.[11] More recently, a less-characteristic dip in annual enrollment growth by 0.5 percent in 2007 slowed overall Medicaid growth that year to 5.4 percent, even though per-enrollee spending grew by 6.0 percent. Since then, the pace of enrollment growth has become a larger factor in driving Medicaid spending growth higher.[12]

Total projected Medicaid spending for medical assistance payments (which does not include the program's administrative costs), however, was expected to grow much more slowly in 2012—increasing only 0.3 percent. Actuaries at the Centers for Medicare and Medicaid Services (CMS) report that this would be the "second slowest growth rate" for such payments in the history of the program.[13]

Although the provisions of the ACA had no significant effect on the one-time slowdown in 2012 in Medicaid spending, that will not remain the case going forward. Medicaid spending over the next 10 years is expected to increase at an average annual rate of 6.4 percent (and at an average annual rate about 1.4 percentage points faster than average annual gross domestic product growth of 5 percent). The largest share of this spending growth will be due to an annual rate of increase in enrollment of 3.4 percent, reflecting the expansion of Medicaid eligibility under the ACA.[14]

To put these past trends and future estimates within a broader context, it is reasonable to conclude that Medicaid spending will continue to grow as a share of state and federal budgets, as well as the overall economy. However, its cost per enrollee will not drive this growth. Rather, its substantial increase in future enrollees will. In fact, federal budget analysts at the Congressional Budget Office (CBO), CMS, and Congress expect the new Medicaid enrollees to be relatively healthier, younger, and less costly to cover. State governments facing serious budgetary pressures of their own have demonstrated that they will continue to find every way possible to reduce their costs per enrollee. If one assumes that Medicaid programs can continue to reimburse health care providers at rates substantially below those for private insurance and even Medicare, it helps explain why the architects of the ACA rely so heavily on expansion of "cheaper" Medicaid coverage to reduce the number of uninsured Americans under the law.[15]

IS THE MEDICAID FISCAL REFORM TOOLBOX HALF FULL, OR HALF EMPTY?

The primary concern of most right-of-center Medicaid reform proposals at the congressional level in recent years has involved reducing the burden of current and future Medicaid spending on the budgets of the federal and state governments, and the taxpayers who must finance them. The standard policy reform tool kit usually involves a mix of increasingly tighter budgetary caps on Medicaid spending and delegating more discretion to state governments in how they resize their Medicaid benefits and practices to match slow rates of spending growth in the future. The most common proposal builds on changing the current federal share of Medicaid financing from matching funds into block grants to individual states. Although the level of initial federal contributions may remain similar to (or even somewhat higher than) current budget projections for the early years of such block grants, the federal funding would grow at a lower rate in later years. The block grants would be fixed in amount, and grow over time according to more predictable formulas. Most states would be given greater discretion in how they spend the federal funds for Medicaid purposes—usually through waivers of at least some federal requirements under current law.[16]

The best working example thus far for carrying out the block grant approach usually involves a capped allotment of federal funds through the current FMAP formula to provide states with upfront funding over a predetermined period of time.[17]

Block grants would delink state and federal spending on any portions of Medicaid to which the new funding allocations applied.

Under FMAP rules, the open-ended federal reimbursement of at least half, and often more (the average is 57 percent across all states), of state Medicaid program expenditures has created strong incentives for states to spend less carefully. Each state's Medicaid program ends up larger than it would be if its own taxpayers had to pay the entire cost. This upward long-term bias toward greater state Medicaid spending discourages more timely responsible reforms and pushes state programs beyond their sustainable limits.

Truly meaningful and cost-effective Medicaid reform must begin (but not end) with substantial changes to the financing of Medicaid at the federal level.

FMAP rules in practice, as opposed to in original theory, have rewarded several richer states at the expense of poorer ones and encouraged additional state Medicaid spending on the margin to maximize matching federal dollars.[18] Rearranging the federal share of Medicaid funding into block grants to the states, with future annual updates indexed somewhat below current Medicaid spending growth rate projections, has traditionally provided a formulaic shortcut to dilute those incentives.

Putting Medicaid on a more fixed budget, such as through block grant federal funding, would provide greater budgetary certainty at both levels of government. By knowing the likely amount of federal assistance to expect in future years, state Medicaid programs could be managed more carefully for the long haul. The political appeal behind block-grant-style Medicaid reform is enhanced when it provides more operational discretion to states managing their Medicaid programs.

However, more simplistic block grant reforms that address only federal fiscal problems at the aggregate level would not necessarily solve longstanding Medicaid program problems involving lack of informed choice for beneficiaries, insufficiently vigorous competition in benefits design, and poor incentives for improved health care delivery. And when basic block grant proposals are fleshed out in more detail, they need to resolve more complex issues, such as how current federal funding commitments will be reallocated differently among the states, how generous the block grant support will remain in later years, and what level of current federal guarantees and minimum standards for Medicaid should be maintained.

NECESSARY ADJUSTMENTS

One likely adjustment to broad block grants to the states for Medicaid funding on a fixed budget might involve setting different per capita funding amounts for different categories of Medicaid beneficiaries. This would allow for the total level of federal Medicaid assistance to a state to vary for changes in enrollment levels (such as increased numbers of low-income persons qualifying for Medicaid during recessions) or changes in the mix of Medicaid enrollee types receiving benefits in that state. For example, estimated per capita Medicaid spending in 2011 was $2,851 for children, $4,362 for adults, $15,931 for the elderly, and $17,958 for the disabled.[19] Hence, different levels of per capita block grants might be more appropriate for different types of Medicaid beneficiaries likely to incur, on average, significantly higher or lower health care costs. Should more medically expensive states, with higher underlying health care costs, receive larger per capita block grants? Allowing for too many, or too few, types of adjustments in setting per capita block grants within and across states poses uncertain tradeoffs between need-based payment accuracy and administrative and political feasibility. Whether block grants to states are set at the aggregate or per capita level, they would constitute fairly simple formulas shaped largely by budgetary objectives.

In the best case scenario, initially fixed federal funding under either lump sum or per capita block grants to states will provide them with incentives to be more innovative and efficient in using available resources for their Medicaid programs. If a state spends below the grant, it can use the savings for other areas of need, just like in the Temporary Assistance to Needy Families (TANF) program. However, tighter federal funding limits might instead prove inadequate to provide promised levels of Medicaid services and health care quality. Moreover, simply transferring large amounts of revenue from one level of government responsible for collecting it to another level of government left relatively free to spend it dilutes political accountability for balancing tax decisions with spending ones.

FLEXIBLE MEANS TO ACHIEVE ACCOUNTABLE OUTCOMES

Greater emphasis on federalism in health policy must travel a two-way street. Each state Medicaid program should be accountable for measured improvement in health care quality, whether through better health outcomes or performance metrics, rather than just for close compliance with federal rules and regulations. The latter often has little if any real impact on the lives of beneficiaries and fails to promote efficiency and cost containment. In a block grant or capped allotment approach to Medicaid reform, the primary role of the federal government should be to ensure true accountability and responsibility on the part of states given greater freedom in spending federal dollars. The federal government should offer every state the opportunity to enter into a simplified compact that sets outcome measures and benchmarks and then requires a participating state to report periodically (perhaps quarterly) on its performance toward them. Federal oversight should be triggered when there is a significant deviation in the reported versus projected performance. The number of measures should be limited to no more than 10 for each dimension of health care: cost, quality, and access. This will simplify or eliminate the state plan approval process, allowing states and their constituents to concentrate more on what matters most: better health outcomes, better value, and lower costs.

The federal government should allow states adopting this option to

- Determine their own eligibility categories and income threshold levels for Medicaid;
- Establish rates and service delivery options;

- Design benefit packages that best meet the demographic, public health, and cultural needs of each state or region (whether that involves adding, deleting, or modifying benefits); and
- Use cost sharing as a way to promote individual responsibility for personal health and wellness.

Congress may also consider providing bonus payments for each state that achieves appropriate benchmarks.

However, even the best versions of block-grant-style Medicaid reform essentially hand off many important Medicaid decisions concerning health benefit levels[20] from one set of government officials at the federal level to other policy makers at the state level. Individual beneficiaries remain largely on the sidelines instead of becoming more engaged and empowered.

DIRECT-TO-CONSUMER MEDICAL EMPOWERMENT

A different, more consumer-focused Medicaid reform would develop a defined-contribution alternative for Medicaid financing and coverage at the individual level. If a Medicaid reform proposal needed to hold taxpayer costs and program eligibility rules relatively more constant, defined-contribution payments to individual beneficiaries could facilitate those goals by allowing the nature, level, and quality of Medicaid's health benefits to become more variable and then more freely selected by Medicaid enrollees.

Defined-contribution payments are made more directly and transparently to beneficiaries than the various mechanisms that divert the amount and nature of defined benefit promises through other third-party intermediaries. Defined contributions aim to empower and encourage consumers and patients to make better health care choices. They are designed to stimulate more innovative and accountable competition by health care providers. And they would provide stronger incentives to save and invest so that we can pay more for health care when it delivers more value, but redirect our resources to other investments in well-being when it delivers less. Although defined-contribution public dollars from taxpayers to support such coverage would be limited, the spending of additional private dollars to enhance or expand coverage would not be restricted. Supplemental benefits (paid for exclusively with private dollars) could vary widely, beyond a baseline definition of core coverage (and its actuarial equivalents) that would be supported in whole or in part through taxpayers' defined contributions.

The better version of defined-contribution health benefits would not just place initial control of how to spend those taxpayer subsidies in the hands of beneficiaries; it also would provide an enhanced infrastructure of health information and connections to intermediary agents to assist those beneficiaries in making their health care choices more actionable and effective. This approach would reward insurers, health care providers, and state policy makers for raising the quality of health care, the value of health benefits, and the satisfaction of Medicaid patients instead of just for keeping the apparent costs of the program lower (or hidden).

States pursuing more market-based, consumer-choice reforms also should acknowledge that they may have to decide to cover fewer people, leave more details of health spending decisions to those beneficiaries that are ready and eager to make them, pay participating health care providers for the full costs of care, and measure quality of delivered care more accurately.

MEETING THE FEASIBILITY TEST

The limitations in using simple formulas to schedule budgetary reductions in the future rate of Medicaid spending is that this expedient device may not be politically sustainable if it does not realistically ensure other types of insurance coverage for low-income Americans.

For example, one theoretically appealing concept would replace both traditional Medicaid assistance and the tax preference for employer-sponsored insurance with defined-contribution payments for both kinds of insurance. This could open up new possibilities for explicit and beneficial coordination between the Medicaid program and the coverage normally offered to working-age Americans.

A particularly ambitious approach might restructure taxpayers' financial contributions to health insurance coverage so that all working-age Americans and their families receive a baseline amount of support. It might be set as equal to their proportionate share of the value of eliminating the current exclusion of employer-paid premiums from federal income and payroll taxes. In most past formulations of this proposal, a fixed, refundable tax credit would be paid to all American households. That could be explicitly amended to include those who otherwise would also be eligible for Medicaid (most likely just those who are nonelderly and not disabled).[21] Medicaid funds could then supplement this financing mechanism for those with especially low incomes who need additional support beyond that base amount (from the reallocated funds of the tax exclusion) to pay for more of their remaining premiums and cost sharing, perhaps delivered through a specially dedicated health savings account. These add-on Medicaid payments could then be phased down gradually to avoid producing substantial disincentives for the beneficiaries to climb the wage and income ladder on their own.

Integration of the taxpayer-provided financial assistance side of health coverage would then allow better coordination and more portable insurance for low-income families who also work. One possible enhanced feature might give states an incentive to develop specific insurance selection structures that allow Medicaid beneficiaries to enroll in the same kinds of plans as workers with higher wages. To reap the benefits of moving toward a defined-contribution system based on full consumer choice of competing plans offering different models for accessing services, Medicaid participants would have a greater share of their premiums subsidized by the combined tax credit and a substantial portion of the Medicaid payments for which they previously were eligible. But those beneficiaries still would face some additional costs if they chose to enroll in more expensive coverage options.

If current (pre-ACA) Medicaid support payments were converted into such defined-contribution payments for a state's nondisabled and nonelderly enrollees, those beneficiaries could be folded into the same insurance selection model as many other state residents. This would give those Medicaid beneficiaries coverage they could retain even as they move up the wage ladder, thus avoiding disruptions in care for themselves and their spouses and children, while putting pressure on the plans to offer value and quality to keep them as paying customers.

STRETCHING THE LIMITS OF PREMIUM ASSISTANCE?

Of course, states have been granted authority already, if they choose to exercise it, to use Medicaid funds to subsidize the purchase of private health insurance for eligible beneficiaries, such as coverage sponsored by their employer, through premium assistance programs. At least 39 states operate some form of premium assistance through Medicaid or CHIP. States have the option to use wraparound coverage that supplements an employer's health plan benefits and pays for some or all of its cost sharing and thereby delivers the same coverage as any other beneficiary in the states' traditional Medicaid programs.

However, enrollees in such options account for less than 1 percent of total Medicaid/CHIP enrollment and an even smaller portion of those two programs' spending.[22] Among the impediments to greater use of premium assistance are federal and state price controls that shift costs to private payers.[23] Such premium assistance also must maneuver through complex and costly administrative procedures. Lack of affordable (or any) employer-sponsored coverage for many low-income workers, on the one hand, or employers' concern that additional enrollment will increase their own health plan costs, on the other hand, further limit the potential of premium assistance.

Other proposals to privatize a substantial portion of current Medicaid coverage with equal or better private health insurance must overcome equally challenging cost–benefit tests. Simply comparing and then trying to match the costs of Medicaid versus private coverage for different populations and different mixes of benefits, let alone different coverage arrangements, remains a daunting policy reform challenge. For example, CBO projected in July 2012 that, under the ACA, the average new enrollee in Medicaid would cost taxpayers roughly $6,000 a year by 2022, whereas the average new enrollee in the ACA's heavily subsidized health exchanges would cost $9,000 a year (50 percent more).[24]

A different estimate in November 2012 by Urban Institute analysts noted that the cost of covering a new Medicaid enrollee varies by the individual's health status, previous coverage, and other characteristics, as well as by changes in prices for medical services over time. Allowing for those caveats, they estimated that the resulting average cost per Medicaid enrollee would rise from $5,440 in 2016 to $7,399 in 2022.[25]

Comparison with the cost of coverage on the private insurance side depends on which segment of that market one uses as an alternative and whether one accounts for significant differences between private insurance and Medicaid in what is officially covered, who enrolls, and what is actually delivered. Average premium costs in the individual market were $2,580 per year in 2011, and average premiums in the employer group market (for individual coverage) were $5,615 per year in 2012.[26] However, benefit packages are significantly more generous in the employer market than in the individual market, and the former are generally subject to lower percentages of out-of-pocket cost sharing.

In examining proposals to provide equal or better coverage to current Medicaid enrollees through subsidized private insurance alternatives, one must ask several preliminary questions before assessing the relative net costs to taxpayers and to enrollees:

Which type of Medicaid population is involved? Mothers with children, kids under 18, and single adults generally are in good health and relatively inexpensive to cover under Medicaid. Annual health care costs and insurance risk premiums for disabled and elderly adults are much higher and less predictable in both the public and private insurance sectors.

How equivalent are the benefits offered in Medicaid versus alternative private coverage? Medicaid officially offers more comprehensive benefits in many cases, with virtually no cost sharing. But its substantially lower reimbursement rates for health care providers also mean that its beneficiaries' access to high-quality health care is much more limited, even if their official per enrollee costs are lower.

Hence, when one assesses the relative merits of more Medicaid coverage versus greater reliance on subsidized private insurance coverage for low-income Americans, ultimate political judgments may hinge more on qualitative and normative factors than on questionable estimates of potential budget savings.

BEYOND BUDGETARY BALANCE SHEETS? IMPROVING HEALTH CARE DELIVERY

Most right-of-center Medicaid reform proposals pay too little attention to improving the quality and value of health care delivered to the program's enrollees. In part, this reflects a healthy deference to the role of private markets and health care practitioners in addressing such problems. But it also indicates a tendency to bypass the thorny details of how to deliver better health care despite budgetary constraints. Once the aggregate fiscal numbers for a formulaic reform approach can be projected to be lower, and the Medicaid program can be painted with a broad brush as a dismal failure,[27] the political temptation is to stop there. But falling back on clichés and nostrums that salute the potential benefits of greater use of managed care, more consumer engagement, and wider discretion for state-level managers of Medicaid programs—without more concrete plans to implement them—is far from enough to constitute meaningful reform.

Managed care for an increased share of Medicaid beneficiaries is not any sort of universal cure-all. Its effects on costs and quality depend on how well it is executed in practice, as well as the setting in which it occurs. The standard managed-care tool kit for reducing Medicaid costs on the health care delivery side (besides paying providers less) is well known in theory but more difficult to implement consistently:

- Move more health care treatment encounters to less-sophisticated settings and lower-cost providers
- Keep beneficiaries out of the higher-cost hospitals, emergency rooms, and nursing homes as much as possible
- Catch potential health problems sooner through preventive care, early diagnoses, and better coordination across multiple health care providers
- Ensure that Medicaid funding follows the beneficiary across the multiple settings where they need and choose care, rather than locking them into more siloed care-delivery processes

Medicaid program contracts with managed care providers, in theory, offer a mechanism to hold participating health plans or providers more accountable for the health outcomes and patient experience of Medicaid enrollees through various performance standards. A recent 50-state survey of Medicaid managed care programs by the Kaiser Commission on Medicaid and the Uninsured indicates that states are increasingly mandating managed care for previously exempt or excluded Medicaid beneficiaries, and that such programs already cover about two-thirds of all Medicaid beneficiaries.[28] Broader efforts to focus managed care on dual eligibles are expanding or getting under way. These projected expansions are driven by both severe state budget pressures and interest in improving health care access and quality for Medicaid beneficiaries. The ACA also encourages multiple experiments with expanded managed care interventions for various Medicaid subpopulations.

A cautionary note comes from a recent study by Duggan and Hayford that examined detailed data on state Medicaid expenditures from 1991 to 2003.[29] They found that shifting Medicaid recipients from traditional fee-for-service benefits programs into Medicaid managed care programs did not reduce Medicaid spending in the typical state. Effects of the shift varied significantly across states as a function of the relative generosity of the state's baseline Medicaid provider reimbursement rates. In states where Medicaid provider reimbursement is very low relative to commercial reimbursement rates, managed care contracting seemed to increase Medicaid spending, and vice versa. The likely explanation is that most managed care programs achieve their savings primarily through obtaining lower prices rather than reducing quantities of health care services. Duggan and Hayford acknowledge that elderly and disabled Medicaid recipients may differ in many respects from most of the Medicaid recipients previously affected by managed care mandates. However, given that current and future Medicaid reimbursement rates appear to be moving downward because of severe budgetary pressures and few other cost-reducing options available for state policy makers, their overall analysis suggests that the potential for further future savings from Medicaid managed care is increasingly limited.

BUILDING A BETTER POLITICAL NARRATIVE FOR MEDICAID REFORM

Assembling an effective coalition in favor of more market-based alternatives to expansion of an unreformed Medicaid program will require more than a recitation of budget projections that suggest "it costs too much" and "we can't afford it." Those statements may contain accurate mathematical conclusions, but they fail to offer better, realistic alternatives that can address the health care needs of low-income Americans more effectively.

The political case for Medicaid reform needs to reflect the core values of the political constituencies that will support it. Hence, it needs to combine firm commitments to provide financial assistance to the most vulnerable Americans with greater reliance on more decentralized, market-based choice and competition to carry out those goals more effectively and efficiently. The ultimate test is whether the health outcomes of the poor are improved by such interventions. Spreading more health care services across a wider base of new beneficiaries further up the income ladder, as the ACA envisions, is more likely to dilute their value. Better targeting of such assistance toward disabled, very low-income, and medically impoverished populations is essential. Able-bodied adults without the resources to pay for basic medical bills may merit short-term financial relief while in extreme duress, but public policy interventions need to be more focused on helping them regain independence and self-sufficiency. Taxpayer-subsidized health coverage should be aimed at establishing a politically acceptable floor below which no one should fall, but individuals subject to short-term economic dislocations or uncomfortable circumstances need to know that their access to better health care in the future is tied to how well they fare eventually in the overall economy. Better jobs and higher incomes, rather than larger taxpayer-subsidized transfer payments, must remain their primary ticket out of unmet medical needs and less satisfactory health care.

Even the most optimistic vision of improvements in Medicaid's health care delivery quality and efficiency must consider the effects of slow or stagnant economic growth, rising levels of disabling health conditions, and lack of improvement in the dependency ratio between working taxpayers and beneficiaries dependent on publicly financed health entitlement programs. Hence, health policy should support broader economic policy incentives to work, save, and invest more effectively so as to protect the most vulnerable Americans without increasing their numbers. One of the strongest arguments for limiting the future growth of Medicaid spending should be how it will free up public and private resources to improve the lives of all Americans, but particularly poorer ones, in more effective ways.

There are also clear fiscal and administrative ceilings on the degree to which current Medicaid beneficiaries can be mainstreamed quickly into higher-quality private insurance coverage by offering defined-contribution subsidies that flow directly to them and their chosen insurer. However attractive this ultimate long-term goal may be, achieving it will either cost more money or cover fewer people than both the ACA and the older Medicaid program pretend to do at cut-rate prices. Better private coverage has to pay health care providers more to deliver better care, and the current level of Medicaid spending—even for the less medically challenged nonelderly, nondisabled portion of its covered population—is far from sufficient to handle the cost of those higher premiums on a large scale.

FACILITATING INNOVATIVE HEALTH CARE FOR LOW-INCOME AMERICA

Thoughtful Medicaid reform still can remove or reduce unnecessary impediments to more innovative approaches for delivering better care to low-income individuals and improving their health outcomes. At a minimum, the Medicaid waiver process for state-level experimentation should be streamlined and made less prone to discretionary political micromanagement.[30] Maintenance of effort requirements in the ACA that have restricted state-level changes in eligibility and benefit rules should be limited to minimum commitments in broad budgetary terms, if not eliminated entirely. Permissible corridors for Medicaid beneficiary cost sharing must be widened even beyond those first allowed under the 2005 Deficit Reduction Act so that more effectively targeted incentives to make better health care choices and adopt healthier behaviors can be signaled to a broader mix of Medicaid enrollees.[31] A thoughtful set of additional state-based Medicaid reform recommendations by the Republican Governors Public Policy Committee includes providing states with enhanced options to reward individuals who participate in health promotion or disease prevention activities, and to offer value-added or additional services for individuals choosing a lower-cost plan. The committee's health care task force also called for a necessary reexamination of obsolete federal Medicaid rules for mandatory versus optional benefits.[32]

CONCLUSION

The ACA will overload and stress an already troubled Medicaid program. Medicaid was nearing a fiscal and operational crisis even before this latest attempt to expand the health insurance program for low-income Americans. Moving a modernized Medicaid program beyond its mistakes of the past and ACA-implemented future will require sustainable, substantive reforms that must include more than fiscal spending cap formulas, block grants to state branches of the Medicaid bureaucracy, and overreliance on private managed care contractors to achieve unprecedented cost savings and productivity gains.

The lower bounds of necessary reform certainly include realistic limits on taxpayers' commitments to finance necessary health care services for low-income Americans. But they also need more flexible tradeoffs and better targeting of scarce resources. Those objectives are accomplished best through decentralized decision making, market-based delivery mechanisms, and more transparent accountability.

The upper bounds of Medicaid reform suggest that the program would perform better by concentrating more on its core mission of ensuring improved health outcomes for those most in need. This should involve a broader focus on other areas of public policy that shape the magnitude and nature of the demand for its assistance, as well as the likelihood of the program's success. Although premium assistance models for connecting low-income Medicaid beneficiaries to higher-value private insurance options face substantial fiscal and operational challenges, further experiments with defined-contribution assistance delivered directly to nondisabled, lower-income Americans below age 65 should be encouraged.

NOTES

1. Patient Protection and Affordable Care Act, Pub. L. No. 111-148, 124 Stat. 119 (2010) (codified as amended sections of 42 U.S.C.).

2. The early estimates of increased enrollment by the Congressional Budget Office (CBO) varied to some degree within that higher range, depending on when they were issued and the period of time over which they were projected. See, for example, Congressional Budget Office, "Letter to the Honorable Nancy Pelosi providing an estimate of the direct spending and revenue effects of an amendment in the nature of a substitute to H.R. 4872, the Reconciliation Act of 2010," March 20, 2010 (estimating about 16 million more enrollees in Medicaid and CHIP by fiscal year 2019 above the pre-ACA baseline), http://www.cbo.gov/sites/default/files/cbofiles/ftpdocs/113xx/doc11379/amendreconprop.pdf; and Congressional Budget Office, "Updated Estimates for the Insurance Coverage Provisions of the Affordable Care Act," March 2012 (estimating from 16 million to 17 million more individuals covered by Medicaid and CHIP during fiscal year 2016 through fiscal year 2022, than under pre-ACA law), http://cbo.gov/sites/default/files/cbofiles/attachments/03-13-Coverage%20Estimates.pdf.

3. The Supreme Court ruled in *National Federation of Independent Business v. Sebelius* that the federal government could not penalize states that chose not to implement the new health law's original mandate that all state Medicaid programs cover legal residents with incomes up to 138 percent of the federal poverty level (FPL). CBO subsequently lowered its ACA-related Medicaid coverage estimates, projecting a smaller increase—of about 11 million—in enrollees in Medicaid and CHIP by fiscal year 2022. Congressional Budget Office, "Estimates for the Insurance Coverage Provisions of the Affordable Care Act Updated for the Recent Supreme Court Decision," July 2012, http://www.cbo.gov/sites/default/files/cbofiles/attachments/43472-07-24-2012-CoverageEstimates.pdf.

4. See, for example, Avik Roy, "How Medicaid Harms the Poor: A Counter-Rebuttal, Part II," *Apothecary* [serial on the Internet], March 10, 2011, http://www.forbes.com/sites/aroy/2011/03/10/how-medicaid-harms-the-poor-a-counter-rebuttal-part-ii.

5. Will Fox and John Pickering, "Hospital & Physician Cost Shift: Payment Level Comparison of Medicare, Medicaid, and Commercial Payers," Milliman Client Report, December 2008, http://www.milliman.com/expertise/healthcare/publications/rr/pdfs/hospital-physician-cost-shift-RR12-01-08.pdf.

6. See, for example, Kathleen M. King and Kay L. Daly, US Government Accountability Office, *Medicare and Medicaid Fraud, Waste, and Abuse: Effective Implementation of Recent Laws and Agency Actions Could Help Reduce Improper Payments*, GAO-11-409T, Statement before the Senate Committee on Homeland Security and Governmental Affairs, Subcommittee on Federal Financial Management, Government Information, Federal Services, and International Security, March 9, 2011; US Government Accountability Office, *Medicaid Integrity Program: CMS Should Take Steps to Eliminate Duplication and Improve Efficiency*, GAO-13-50, November 2012.

7. See, for example, Sandra L. Decker, "In 2011, Nearly One-Third of Physicians Said They Would Not Accept New Medicaid Patients, but Rising Fees May Help," *Health Affairs* 31, no. 8 (2012): 1673–79; Stephen Zuckerman, Aimee F. Williams, and Karen E. Stockley, "Trends in Medicaid Physician Fees, 2003–2008," *Health Affairs*, April 28, 2009: w510–519, http://content.healthaffairs.org/content/28/3/w510.full.pdf; Peter Cunningham, "Physician Reimbursement and Participation in Medicaid," presentation to the Medicaid and CHIP Payment and Access Commission, September 23, 2010, http://www.hschange.com/CONTENT/1157/1157.pdf.

8. A somewhat countervailing dynamic will be produced by a so-called "woodwork" effect that might encourage greater enrollment of individuals eligible for Medicaid under pre-ACA rules (and at lower matching rates for federal funding). This would be due to the effects of the ACA's individual coverage mandate, expanded health insurance enrollment efforts, and streamlined Medicaid eligibility rules.

9. Office of the Actuary, US Department of Health & Human Services, 2012 *Actuarial Report on the Financial Outlook for Medicaid*, March 2013, 17, http://www.medicaid.gov/Medicaid-CHIP-Program-Information/By-Topics/Financing-and-Reimbursement/Downloads/medicaid-actuarial-report-2012.pdf.

10. Ibid., 48.

11. For example, Medicaid spending grew relatively more slowly—at a 6.4 annual average rate—from 1994 through 1999; largely because Medicaid enrollment growth decelerated dramatically (below population growth rates), after a series of program eligibility expansions in the early 1990s. The main factors behind the enrollment growth slowdown from 1994 through 1999 were strong economic growth and welfare reform. However, Medicaid spending growth picked up speed from 2000 through 2005, increasing at an average of 8.8 percent per year. Most of that was due to annual enrollment growth of 6.3 percent, whereas Medicaid spending per enrollee grew at only 2.4 percent a year. Ibid., 18.

12. In 2008, Medicaid enrollment grew 2.7 percent, contributing to a 5.9 percent increase in Medicaid spending. The effects of enrollment growth (6.7 percent) were even greater in 2009, when overall Medicaid spending increased by 7.6 percent. A somewhat slower rate of Medicaid spending growth in 2010 (up 6.1 percent from 2008) still was driven largely by enrollment increasing by 5.5 percent. Even when Medicaid spending picked up slightly in 2011 (growing by 6.4 percent), more of that growth was caused by estimated increases in enrollment (up 3.8 percent) than by increases in Medicaid spending per enrollee (up 2.6 percent). Ibid., 19–20.

13. Although overall health spending growth rates have been noticeably lower in recent years due to the 2007–09 recession and relatively sluggish economic growth since then, the most significant one-time factor in the sudden drop in the Medicaid growth rate in 2012 appears to have been the elimination of recent temporary increases in the federal matching rates of funding for state Medicaid programs for 2009, 2010, and 2011, adopted under the 2009 American Recovery and Reinvestment Act. State policy makers experienced an offsetting short-term surge in the annual rate of increase for their state's Medicaid expenditures (up 19.9 percent in 2011 and 18.1 percent in 2012 from a lower state matching rate base), but they responded by adopting stronger efforts to prevent even faster spending growth. Ibid., 20, 25; Vernon K. Smith et al., "Medicaid Today; Preparing for Tomorrow: A Look at State Medicaid Program Spending, Enrollment and Policy Trends," Henry J. Kaiser Family Foundation, October 2012.

14. Office of the Actuary, 2012 *Actuarial Report*, iv, 50.

15. See Thomas P. Miller, "Only a Cease-Fire in a Political Hundred-Years' War," *Health Affairs* 29 (6): 1101–5; Thomas P. Miller, "Health Reform's Late-Term Delivery: Struggling with Political Birth Defects," American Enterprise Institute Online, June 8, 2010, http://www.aei.org/speech/health/healthcare-reform/health-reforms-late-term-delivery-struggling-with-political-birth-defects/.

16. Waiver authority under current law provides federal government permission for states to test new or existing ways to deliver and pay for health care services. In the Medicaid program, there are four primary types of waivers and demonstration projects for

which states can apply. Section 1115 Research & Demonstration Projects provide states with program flexibility to test particular approaches in financing and delivery of Medicaid benefits. Section 1915(b) Managed Care Waivers allow states to provide services through managed care delivery systems or to otherwise limit beneficiaries' choice of providers. Section 1915(c) Home- and Community-Based Service Waivers permit states to provide long-term care services in home and community settings rather than in institutional settings. With Concurrent Section 1915(b) and 1915(c) Waivers, states can simultaneously implement two types of waivers to provide a continuum of services to the elderly and people with disabilities, as long as all federal requirements for both programs are met.

17. Rhode Island received a Global Medicaid waiver in 2009 to establish a new state–federal compact. In exchange for much more flexibility to run its state Medicaid program, Rhode Island agreed to provide the federal government with greater fiscal certainty. Under the waiver, Rhode Island promised to operate its Medicaid program under an aggregate budget cap of $12.075 billion (combined federal and state spending) over a five year period. The first-of-its-kind Rhode Island agreement capped the federal government's obligations for an entitlement at a fixed level. If the state program spends more than this average trend rate and total spending exceeds the cap, Rhode Island is responsible for 100 percent of those additional costs. The Rhode Island waiver is not a block grant. It preserves the FMAP formula for determining the relative federal share of the total level of the state Medicaid program's spending, but it caps that aggregate spending through 2013. Within these federal funding limits, the state was given greater freedom to design and redesign its program. The early results have been promising. In the first 18 months under the global waiver, estimated savings were $100 million, and the annual rate of growth in total Medicaid spending was reduced by more than half, from 7.94 percent to 3 percent. If the state's Medicaid spending continues on the same path for the next three years, it will amount to several billion dollars less than the cap agreed to for the five-year demonstration. See Tom Miller, "Taking Medicaid Off Steroids," in *The Great Experiment: The States, The Feds and Your Healthcare* (Boston: Pioneer Institute, 2012), 84; and The Lewin Group, *An Independent Evaluation of Rhode Island's Global Waiver* (Falls Church, VA: The Lewin Group, December 2011), 1–3.

18. The higher-income states can afford to expand their programs in prosperous economic times to a greater extent than poorer states, but they cut Medicaid expenditures less when their economies contract. Even though wealthier states have lower matching rates, they have expanded their programs to a greater extent than the states that typically have higher proportions of poor people. Robert B. Helms, "Medicaid: The Forgotten Issue in Health Reform," AEI *Health Policy Outlook* (November 2009), http://www.aei.org/article/health/healthcare-reform/medicaid-the-forgotten-issue-in-health-reform/.

19. Office of the Actuary, *2012 Actuarial Report*, iii.

20. For example: How comprehensive will benefits be? With how much cost-sharing? What degree of medical management will be applied to them?

21. Applying a defined contribution to the costliest and most medically complex Medicaid beneficiaries—the elderly, blind, and disabled, many of whom are dually eligible for Medicare coverage—is more problematic and less practical in the near term. Those categories of Medicaid coverage need more complex, long-term reform approaches that merit a more nuanced discussion beyond the limits of this chapter.

22. Cynthia Shirk, "Premium Assistance: An Update" (Background Paper 80, National Health Policy Forum, October 12, 2010); US Government Accountability Office,

"Medicaid and CHIP: Enrollment, Benefits, Expenditures, and other Characteristics of State Premium Assistance Programs," GAO-10-258R, January 19, 2010.

23. Fox and Pickering, "Hospital and Physician Cost Shift." Federal approval of state premium-assistance plan waivers also requires states to demonstrate their cost-effectiveness compared to traditional state Medicaid coverage and guarantee that they will offer comparable health benefits and protection against cost sharing.

24. Congressional Budget Office, *Estimates for the Insurance Coverage Provisions of the Affordable Care Act Updated for the Recent Supreme Court Decision*, 15–16. The extra exchange costs per person are larger than the decrease in Medicaid costs per person primarily because, in CBO's and the Joint Committee on Taxation's estimation, private health insurance plans in the exchanges will pay providers at higher rates than Medicaid pays and will have higher administrative costs than Medicaid, although there are other, partially offsetting, factors as well.

25. John Holahan et al., "The Cost and Coverage Implications of the ACA Medicaid Expansion: National and State-by-State Analysis," Kaiser Commission on Medicaid and the Uninsured, November 2012.

26. See Henry J. Kaiser Family Foundation, "Average Per Person Monthly Premiums in the Individual Market," State Health Facts, http://kff.org/other/state-indicator/individual-premiums/; The Kaiser Family Foundation and Health Research and Educational Trust, *Employer Health Benefits: 2012 Annual Survey* (2012).

27. For example, note the quick dismissal by many conservative critics of expanded Medicaid coverage on the grounds that its short-term benefits are quite limited, in the wake of recent evidence that it failed to improve several measurable health outcomes compared to other study participants left uninsured. Katherine Baicker et al., "The Oregon Experiment—Effects of Medicaid on Clinical Outcomes," *New England Journal of Medicine* 368, no. 18 (2013): 1713–22.

28. Katherine Gifford et al., "A Profile of Medicaid Managed Care Programs in 2010: Findings from a 50-State Survey," Kaiser Commission on Medicaid and the Uninsured, September 2011, http://www.kff.org/medicaid/upload/8220.pdf.

29. Mark Duggan and Tamara Hayford, "Has the Shift to Managed Care Reduced Medicaid Expenditures? Evidence from State and Local-Level Mandates" (Working Paper 17236, National Bureau of Economic Research), http://www.nber.org/papers/w17236.

30. Fred Upton and Orrin Hatch, *Making Medicaid Work: Protect the Vulnerable, Offer Individualized Care, and Reduce Costs*, United States Congress, May 1, 2013, 10–11, http://energycommerce.house.gov/sites/republicans.energycommerce.house.gov/files/analysis/20130501Medicaid.pdf.

31. The premium and cost-sharing provision under the Deficit Reduction Act of 2005 (DRA) gave states new options to align their Medicaid programs more closely to private insurance plans, such as requiring recipients to pay monthly premiums, deductibles, coinsurance or copayments. Prior to passage of the DRA, Medicaid regulations allowed states to impose nominal cost sharing on certain Medicaid recipients. Premium charges were generally prohibited. Under the DRA, states no longer needed to obtain a waiver from the secretary of the Department of Health and Human Services to impose cost-sharing charges and premiums on certain nonexempt Medicaid recipients. States are now allowed to charge copayments greater than the nominal amount to some Medicaid recipients and premiums to recipients with family incomes above 150 percent of the FPL. In addition, states can require payment of any allowable cost sharing at the point of service before providing care or services for

individuals with income above 100 percent of the FPL. Centers for Medicare and Medicaid Services, "Deficit Reduction Act Important Facts for State Policymakers," February 21, 2008, https://www.cms.gov/Regulations-and-Guidance/Legislation/DeficitReductionAct/Guidance/Legislation/DeficitReductionAct/downloads/Costsharing.pdf.

32. Republican Governors Public Policy Committee Health Care Task Force, "A New Medicaid: A Flexible, Innovative and Accountable Future," 11, 13.

CHAPTER 9: MEDICAID AND HEALTH

ROBERT F. GRABOYES

The expansion of Medicaid is a central component of the Patient Protection and Affordable Care Act (ACA).[1] The law sought to increase the nation's health insurance rolls by approximately 30 million (out of roughly 50 million uninsured). About half of the newly enrolled would themselves be covered not by private insurance, but rather by Medicaid—the country's insurance program for the poor.[2]

The disastrous rollout of healthcare.gov has thrown the ACA's survival into doubt. The entire ACA depends on a vast array of data flows and, in early 2014, it is unclear when or whether the public website will become fully functional. Arguably, regardless of whether the website becomes fully functional, even worse problems await the law.[3] Before anyone imagined the problems with healthcare.gov, there were warnings that the ACA's biggest obstacles would lie in the perpetual need to meld disparate data on every American from an enormous array of public and private databases that have great difficulty interfacing.[4] At the same time, the Supreme Court's 2012 ruling on the ACA[5] greatly weakened the incentives for states to agree to the law's Medicaid expansion, precipitating heated debate in many states over how to proceed.

Given these uncertainties, it is an appropriate time to evaluate the efficacy of Medicaid as an institution capable of improving or maintaining its recipients' health. This chapter examines a growing body of evidence that Medicaid badly fails the enrollees it is designed to help. The program provides poor coverage, poor care, and poor outcomes. Therefore, Medicaid falls into the same category as inner-city public schools and government-run housing projects—hugely expensive social engineering initiatives that often fail their recipients.

An eloquent criticism of the program came in 2009 from Senator Ron Wyden (D-OR), who referred to Medicaid as a "caste system" that limits the ability of the poor to access the providers and care they desire. "I want poor people in this country to have the kind of quality of care and dignity that members of Congress have," he said.[6] On that note, it is worth reviewing some of the key points made by the other authors in this volume.

Joe Antos noted Medicaid's sheer size ($465 billion per year) and rapid growth rate (7 percent per year during 2000–12, versus 4.2 percent gross domestic product growth). Antos also explored the conflicting incentives that allow states to draw funds from other states, but only if they are willing to simultaneously raise their own residents' taxes. Jason Fichtner notes that with 57 million enrollees, Medicaid is the nation's largest health insurer. He, too, describes the tension between the states' beggar-thy-neighbor and beggar-thyself incentives. Nina Owcharenko describes the massive fiscal impact that Medicaid has on the states. Charles Blahous notes the financial risk to state budgets posed by the so-called "woodwork" effect—previously eligible enrollees drawn in by publicity surrounding the expansion. June O'Neill noted that Medicaid has effectively become a long-term care program. James Capretta describes the waiver option that some states have used to improve on the general Medicaid model (e.g., Indiana, Rhode Island, Massachusetts). Darcy Nikol Bryan describes physician–patient interactions in the Medicaid environment.

Thomas Miller's chapter is perhaps the closest in spirit to the present chapter. He examines some of the evidence that Medicaid provides poor coverage, care, and outcomes and warns that Medicaid critics who favor market approaches frequently slide toward complacency and all-too-easy dismissal of Medicaid altogether. He suggests that market advocates need to focus on the quality of care and not just on the fiscal aspects of Medicaid. And he stresses the need for Medicaid's critics to make the case that a more affordable system will more effectively address the health care needs of low-income Americans. He notes that some ideas popular among market advocates (e.g., defined-contribution plans, vouchers, Medicaid managed care) are not panaceas, especially given the particular qualities of Medicaid enrollees. This chapter will build on these authors' insights, and especially on Miller's.

BACK TO BASICS

Medicaid is a means to an end, and the end is (or ought to be) health for lower-income Americans. Health, of course, is not the same as health care or health insurance or access to health insurance, though the distinctions are often forgotten in public policy debates. By and large, the subject of this book thus far has been the means—the institution of Medicaid and its impacts on America's finances. That is an important and appropriate topic, given that Medicaid is vast, deeply imbedded in our economy, a cornerstone of the social safety net, and unlikely to go away anytime in the near future. This final chapter focuses more on the end (health) than on the means (the particulars of Medicaid), and ultimately ponders whether the program ought to be replaced by some other form of low-income assistance.

A Mercatus publication I authored in 2013 stated the following: "An ideal health care system will provide better health to more people at lower cost on a continuous basis."[7] By this standard, Medicaid is an abject failure. For lower-income Americans, Medicaid yields poor coverage, poor care, and poor medical outcomes. While promising coverage far beyond the program's original scope, it fails to enroll millions of people who are among its intended population and who are eligible for enrollment. The data suggest that Medicaid does surprisingly little to improve its recipients' health and in some ways may even harm them indirectly. It is a pennywise-and-pound-foolish program that, paradoxically, sends costs soaring by underpaying providers. And the coverage, care, and cost elements show little or no improvement over time.[8]

Medicaid is problematic both for its recipients and for the taxpayers who underwrite the program. This chapter will explore some of the specific examples of how Medicaid fails with regard to coverage, care, and outcomes for its recipients. It will briefly discuss how the ACA amplifies Medicaid's already considerable negatives, but paradoxically affords an opportunity to steer Medicaid in directions that better serve the health of those in lower-income strata, as well as the rest of the health care system.

MEDICAID PROVIDES POOR COVERAGE

With Medicaid, health care coverage is incomplete and in some cases, tenuous. Because eligibility is based on income and number of people in the household, some people drift in and out of coverage as their incomes and family sizes undulate. And expansion of eligibility can lead to mass cancellations of coverage when the financial costs prove infeasible.

Medicaid currently has approximately 57 million enrollees.[9] But about 11 million individuals are eligible for Medicaid but are not enrolled.[10] The eligible-but-not-enrolled comprise about 16 percent of the Medicaid-eligible population and 25 percent of America's uninsured.[11] Coincidentally the uninsured portion of those eligible for Medicaid is similar to the uninsured portion of the American public in general (about 16 percent).[12] In a certain sense, the eligible-but-not-enrolled are de facto covered in that they can enroll retroactively, thereby covering expenses incurred while the potential enrollees are technically uninsured. Of course, the eligible-but-not-enrolled may behave differently with respect to care. It is more difficult to say whether that altered behavior harms or helps the unenrolled.

The ACA aims to expand Medicaid enrollment by roughly 15 million individuals.[13] But eligibility is based on the federal poverty level (FPL) and therefore depends both on income and on the number of people in a household. Changes in either variable can shift individuals or families into or out of eligibility. Given the volatility of income among lower-income Americans, this can lead to "churn"—drifting in and out of coverage as family circumstances change over time. In 2011, Sommers and Rosenbaum, both supporters of the ACA, estimated the amount of churn that would be experienced in a fully realized ACA expansion of Medicaid (up to 138 percent of FPL). They estimated that over a given year, 50 percent of adults below 200 percent of FPL (28 million individuals) would experience a shift from the exchanges into Medicaid or vice versa.[14] They further predicted that some would see two, three, or even four or more shifts in a given year and suggested that such churn would likely lead to discontinuities in care.[15] Sommers and Rosenbaum expressed concern that individuals experiencing such churn might tire of the shifts and stop maintaining coverage or seeking care.[16]

Rapid expansion of Medicaid, as envisioned under the ACA, also has the potential to touch off a cycle of expansion, financial overload, and mass cancellations of coverage. The best example of such a process is the TennCare disaster that began in 1994 in Tennessee. The state sought to convert Medicaid to managed care, assuming this would lead to enough savings (from efficiency gains) to cover children and the uninsured. In less than a decade, however, enrollment swelled far beyond what had been predicted, and the savings proved elusive. The expansion threatened the state government with bankruptcy and, by 2006, the program was forced to cancel coverage for approximately 200,000 Tennesseans.[17] A high-profile study of Oregon's Medicaid expansion provides powerful new evidence that expansion increases rather than decreases the use of emergency services; putting it another way, one of the principal arguments in favor of expansion now appears illusory.[18]

In sum, Medicaid has a longstanding problem enrolling those who are eligible. The eligibility requirements can lead to instability in a household's coverage, and there is some susceptibility to large-scale cancellations of coverage.

MEDICAID PROVIDES POOR CARE

Once one is enrolled in Medicaid, access to quality care becomes a serious challenge. Because of low reimbursement rates and other factors, many providers do not accept Medicaid patients; others may retain existing Medicaid patients but decline new ones. Excess demand by Medicaid enrollees requires rationing, which occurs in several ways, including discouragement by wait times and by political allocation of care. The end result is frequent and medically suboptimal use of emergency rooms outside of the desired Medicaid channels.

Medicaid represents a classic shortage market. Providers are compensated less by Medicaid than they would be in a free-market equilibrium. In fact, Medicaid generally pays among the lowest reimbursement rates of any health insurance program.[19] Providers are also discouraged from accepting Medicaid patients by long delays in receiving their reimbursement funds and by the fact that Medicaid patients require more provider time and resources on average than many other classes of patients.[20] As a result, providers often experience financial losses when treating a Medicaid patient. At the same time, Medicaid patients pay even less, or receive care at no out-of-pocket expense. As in any market, if consumer and producer prices are set below equilibrium levels, there will be excess demand and, hence, the need to ration allocation by nonmonetary methods. This problem will likely only become exacerbated with the expansion of Medicaid under the ACA.

During 2011–12, roughly one-third of physicians declined to accept new Medicaid patients.[21] The problem is not improving.[22] During 2003–08, Medicaid's reimbursement rates rose by less than the general rate of inflation—thus implying a real reduction in the already low compensation level (equal to 72 percent of that of Medicare).[23] The ACA included temporary increases in Medicaid reimbursement rates, but the rollout of even those temporary increases has been problematic. The increase, planned for early 2013, has experienced delays.[24] The ACA's reimbursement increase, set to last two years, would increase reimbursement rates up to Medicare levels; but states have been slow to implement these rate increases, and the change remains in question.[25] The delays have resulted from slow rollout of federal regulations and slow responses by state authorities.[26] In California, where Medicaid enrollment is expected to rise from seven million to nine million, reimbursement rates are low and are being cut still further.[27] In 2012, the Texas Medical Association reported that only 31 percent of Texas physicians will accept new Medicaid patients, citing red-tape and administrative burdens as important causes.[28]

Medicaid recipients often face substantial wait times for care, and the nonmonetary cost of waiting discourages some from seeking care.[29] One result of these resource shortages is that Medicaid patients often seek routine and other care in emergency rooms rather than in far less expensive settings—such as doctors' offices. Emergency room visits increased in Massachusetts after the state's 2006 health care reform ("Romneycare"[30]) became law.[31] Many expect the situation to worsen nationally as the ACA expands the Medicaid rolls with no commensurate increase in provider resources.[32,33]

But rationing also occurs by political means. States limit the types of procedures and providers to be compensated. The Medicaid program in Oregon has perhaps the most sophisticated of these state allocation systems, and that state's experience with rationing provides some of the more vivid examples of the moral challenges of rationing of care via politics.

Up through 1985, reimbursement for transplants was determined on a case-by-case basis. Beginning in 1985, however, Congress required a more systematic process for approving and disapproving reimbursement. In a celebrated case in 1987, seven-year-old Coby Howard was diagnosed with a form of leukemia. The only available treatment was a $100,000 bone marrow transplant, which was not covered under the state's post-1985 plan. The child's plight became the subject of intense nationwide publicity and lobbying efforts to alter the plan's restrictions. While the child's death ultimately rendered the controversy moot, in the heat of the controversy there were legislative proposals to reverse the regulation. Ted Koppel, host of ABC's Nightline program, asked the following on-air: "Is the cost of modern medical technology forcing public officials to play God?"[34]

After the Coby Howard controversy, Oregon moved toward an overt rationing plan modeled somewhat on the procedures used by Britain's National Health Service. The state assembled panels of experts—doctors, consumer advocates, health care administrators, and medical ethics experts—to determine how the state's Medicaid program would limit its payouts.[35] The result was that 1,600 medical procedures were ranked by a measure of how much health would be provided by one dollar of expenditure; to put it in the vernacular, procedures were ranked by how much bang for the buck each provided.[36] Across this list, the state figuratively drew a line; the allegedly high-value procedures above the line would be covered, whereas those below would not. The line was drawn in such a way as to balance the cost of the above-the-line procedures with the state's global Medicaid budget.[37] The rationing system again made national headlines in 2008; Oregon Medicaid does not reimburse treatments such as chemotherapy if medical authorities determine that the procedure will have less than a 5 percent probability of success. In 2008, Oregon Medicaid declined to cover cancer treatments for 64-year-old Barbara Wagner but, instead, sent her a letter offering coverage of assisted suicide services.[38]

Aside from other moral questions, programs like Oregon's raise a serious question: Will ad hoc rationing (as during the Coby Howard episode) or algorithmic rationing (as in the later period) bias care and resources toward diseases that especially afflict the well connected and the telegenic?

In sum, as a market perpetually in a state of excess demand, Medicaid is forced to ration care. Whether intentionally or not, the excess demand is reduced as wait times and other inconveniences increase. However, as the Oregon example shows, rationing can also be overt and political.

MEDICAID PROVIDES POOR OUTCOMES

The beginning of this chapter stressed that Medicaid's goal ought to be health, rather than health insurance or health care. It is in this realm that the evidence against Medicaid is most powerful. Glenn Reynolds,[39] Avik Roy,[40] and Scott Gottlieb[41] provide excellent overviews of the program's dismal record in improving people's health. A Heritage Foundation study examined data related to the TennCare disaster described above. The study found that even after TennCare's explosive increase in costs, Tennessee's mortality rate did not improve vis-à-vis neighboring states.[42] A large and growing academic literature documents situations in which Medicaid recipients fare no better than or fare even worse than the uninsured. The following are some of the more prominent of these studies:

A 2008 Columbia–Cornell study showed that uninsured and Medicaid patients had a higher risk of certain serious cardiovascular conditions than people with other types of insurance; among those treated, the differences were mostly absent, suggesting that access to care was the key difference.[43] A 1999 University of Florida study indicated that, along with the uninsured, Medicaid recipients' cancers are diagnosed later than those of individuals with other forms of insurance.[44] A 2011 study in *Cancer* showed Medicaid patients' survival rates to be lower than those insured by other plans.[45] A 2010 University of Pittsburgh study found that "Patients with Medicaid/uninsured and Medicare disability were at increased risk of death after a diagnosis of [head and neck cancer] when compared with patients with private insurance, after adjustment for age, gender, race, smoking, alcohol use, site, socioeconomic status, treatment, and cancer stage."[46]

In 2010, the University of Virginia conducted a large-scale study that suggested that an individual without insurance has better health outcomes than an individual on Medicaid.[47] Even after adjusting for risk factors, Medicaid patients had higher in-hospital mortality, longer hospital stays, and higher costs—compared with the uninsured, those on Medicare, and those on private insurance plans.[48] A University of Pennsylvania study examined data on patients receiving surgery for colorectal cancer; Medicaid patients had higher mortality and surgical complications than uninsured patients.[49] A 2011 Johns Hopkins study found that "Medicare and Medicaid patients have worse survival after [lung transplantation] compared with private insurance/self-paying patients."[50]

Perhaps the most damning of all the recent studies is the Oregon Experiment.[51] This was a rare example of a large-scale, fully randomized experiment in health care. In 2008, Oregon expanded its Medicaid program. Approximately 90,000 people applied for 30,000 newly available slots, and the state used a lottery to choose who got in and who did not. Afterward, the state tracked the health of 6,387 adults who were chosen and 5,842 who were not. From a standpoint of physical health, the results were devastating: "This randomized, controlled study showed that Medicaid coverage generated no significant improvements in measured physical health outcomes in the first 2 years, but it did increase use of health care services, raise rates of diabetes detection and management, lower rates of depression, and reduce financial strain." Supporters of Medicaid point to positives that follow the word "but" in the preceding sentence.

None of this evidence suggests that Medicaid harms its enrollees' overall health; in fact, there is a strong case to suggest that, other things being equal, it is better to be on Medicaid than to be uninsured. But the lack of improvement in physical health metrics strongly bolsters the case that whatever its merits, Medicaid is deeply substandard in providing its recipients with health.

WHERE TO GO

The growing body of ambiguous evidence ought to raise questions about how America provides the poor with health care. One can strongly support the idea of a social safety net without assuming that the present-day incarnation of Medicaid is the only option. This final section offers some thoughts.

Several dozen states have rushed pell-mell into the ACA's Medicaid expansion, and many or most others at least feel some pressure to do likewise. The ACA leaves states in a difficult situation. The ACA offers the states two choices: Fully expand coverage to households with incomes up to 138 percent of FPL, or leave things as they are. Special pressure comes from one provision of the ACA. Subsidized insurance exchange policies are available only for those households with incomes above 100 percent of FPL. But in some states, Medicaid eligibility ends well below that 100 percent figure. In Virginia, for example, a couple with children is eligible for Medicaid as long as their income is at or below 31 percent of FPL. The ACA essentially offers Virginia two choices. Expand Medicaid all the way to 138 percent. Or leave those parents whose income lies between 31 percent and 100 percent of FPL without Medicaid and without private insurance subsidies. In other words, in order to cover the 31–100 percent group, the state effectively ends up denying the 100–138 percent group access to federal subsidies with which to purchase private insurance on the exchanges; practically speaking, that means denying them private insurance and moving them into Medicaid.[52]

Expansion advocates offer a moral argument for expansion—failure to do so would leave those in the 31–100 percent range without access to either Medicaid or to private insurance.[53] But there is an equally strong moral argument in the opposite direction. As we have seen, it is difficult to argue that distributing Medicaid cards among the 31–100 percent group will actually improve their health. On the other hand, expansion would mean that the 100–138 percent group would be shifted out of private insurance and shifted into Medicaid.

And the evidence is strong that doing so would be detrimental to their coverage, care, and health.

An added complication is the so-called "woodwork effect." Under the ACA, the federal government is supposed to finance 100 percent of the expansion for three years. The federal share is then to taper off to 90 percent by 2020. However, this funding formula covers only those newly eligible for Medicaid. No doubt, the expansion will bring in some of the previously eligible-but-unenrolled, and they will not attract the federal funds allocated for the expansion; the states will have to pick up the tab for that portion of the expansion.[54]

In "The American Health Care System: Principles for Successful Reform," I described an appropriate strategic goal for health care as follows:

> An ideal health care system will provide better health to more people at lower cost on a continuous basis. This should be the ultimate goal of health care reform. Yet decades of legislative attempts have failed to achieve this aim. Why?
>
> **First,** proposed and enacted reforms have tended to focus on the provision of services rather than on the outcomes of those services.
>
> **Second,** reforms have tended to reinforce the weaknesses of the current system. Existing laws, regulations, institutions, and politics obstruct and discourage cost-cutting innovation. They unnecessarily constrain the supply of care, the means to improve it, and the capacity to lower costs. These problems predate the Affordable Care Act (ACA), but the ACA compounds them. Unfortunately, proponents of market-based solutions have mostly offered piecemeal fixes that have failed to convince broader constituencies.

> **Third,** Washington has aimed far too low. We should not seek to "bend the cost curve," but rather to break it to bits. Enabling more people to receive better care at lower cost on a continuous basis requires replicating the plunging costs and soaring quality in computing, transportation, agriculture, manufacturing, distribution, and communication. In the mid-1990s, simple cell phones were toys of the rich; 15 years later, smartphones dotted the world's poorest villages. When American health care boasts the cost-cutting innovation we associate with a Steve Jobs or Henry Ford, we'll be on the right track.[55]

A common suggestion among market advocates is to move Medicaid to block grants. A more radical suggestion is to restructure the program to meld today's Medicaid recipients into the private insurance market. This is not uniquely an idea of the political right. The Wyden-Bennett bill in 2007 would have phased out Medicaid, and shifted the enrollees into private insurance.[56] Sommers and Rosenbaum[57] suggested relieving the churn problem by creating dual plans for both Medicaid and the insurance exchanges. Arkansas agreed to the ACA's Medicaid expansion by this method, and it has been described favorably by Rosenbaum and Sommers.[58] The *New York Times* noted proposals to expand Medicaid via private insurance.[59] Thomas Miller's chapter in this volume suggests that these ideas are not panaceas. But panaceas are not likely in the offing.

Ultimately, the closest we can come to a panacea is likely to come from disruptive innovation. In a previous article, I noted that for the past 50 years, we may well have been closing off our pathways to medical innovation.[60] In another article, I said the following:

> American health care has no Steve Jobs or Bill Gates. No Jeff Bezos, Elon Musk, Burt Rutan, or Henry Ford. No innovator whose genius and sweat deliver the twin lightning bolts of cost-reduction and quality improvement

> across the broad landscape of health care. Why not? Either we answer that question soon and uncork the genie, or we consign our health care to a prolonged, unaffordable stagnation.[61]

Cost-cutting innovation is probably the best path available for bringing better health to America's poor—and America's not-poor as well. The Medicaid program as currently constituted likely discourages any such innovation. And Medicaid is not unique in that respect.

Medicaid was created in 1965 to provide medical coverage for the poor. As is now clear, coverage does not necessarily translate into care, and Medicaid's care does not necessarily translate into better health. For the federal and state governments, the program is pricey. For enrollees who navigate Medicaid's labyrinth on the way to care, it is perplexing. And in terms of improving health, it is poor. From a moral standpoint, lower-income Americans deserve a better system than the current one, which is pricey, perplexing, and poor. To improve their lot, we will have to harness private market incentives—either within Medicaid or within a more appropriate replacement structure. For the moment, the ACA is pushing in the opposite direction—expanding a broken program, exacerbating the existing problems, and delaying the onset of more effective, more humane reforms.

NOTES

1. Patient Protection and Affordable Care Act, Pub. L. No. 111-148, 124 Stat. 119 (2010) (codified as amended sections of 42 U.S.C.).
2. It is somewhat incorrect to use the term "newly enrolled," since some of those added to the Medicaid rolls would be people who previously had private insurance.
3. Robert Graboyes, "If They Ever Fix the Obamacare Website, the Worst May Be Yet to Come," *Forbes*, October 31, 2013, http://www.forbes.com/sites/realspin/2013/10/31/if-they-ever-fix-the-obamacare-website-the-worst-may-be-yet-to-come/.
4. C. Eugene Steuerle, "Can the New Health Subsidies Be Administered? The Government We Deserve," November 23, 2009, http://www.urban.org/publications/901303.html; Paul Howard and Stephen T. Parente, "Built to Fail: Health Insurance Exchanges Under the Affordable Care Act (Guest Opinion)," June 15, 2011,

http://www.kaiserhealthnews.org/Columns/2011/June/061511howardparente.aspx.

5. National Federation of Independent Business v. Sebelius 132 S. Ct. 2566.
6. Mary Agnes Casey, "Hot-Button Health Issue: Is Medicaid or Private Insurance Better for the Poor Uninsured?," *Kaiser Health News*, July 1, 2009, http://www.kaiserhealthnews.org/Stories/2009/July/01/Medicaid.aspx?p=1.
7. Robert Graboyes, "The American Health Care System: Principles for Successful Reform" (Arlington, VA: Mercatus Center at George Mason University, October 14, 2013), http://mercatus.org/publication/american-health-care-system-principles-successful-reform.
8. See, for example, Fichtner chapter in this book.
9. Fichtner chapter in this book.
10. Holahan, Cook, and Dubay, Kaiser Commission on Medicaid and the Uninsured, "Characteristics of the Uninsured: Who Is Eligible for Public Coverage and Who Needs Help Affording Coverage?," February 2007, http://kaiserfamilyfoundation.files.wordpress.com/2013/01/7613.pdf.
11. Ibid.
12. Ibid. 57 million have enrolled in Medicaid, and roughly 11 million have not. 11/(11+57)=16.2%. Roughly 50 million people in touch are uninsured, out of a US population of 310 million; 50/310=16.1%.
13. "Status of the ACA Medicaid Expansion after Supreme Court Ruling," Washington, DC: Center on Budget and Policy Priorities, October 22, 2013, http://www.cbpp.org/files/status-of-the-ACA-medicaid-expansion-after-supreme-court-ruling.pdf.
14. Benjamin Sommers and Sara Rosenbaum, "Issues in Health Reform: How Changes in Eligibility May Move Millions Back and Forth Between Medicaid and Insurance Exchanges," *Health Affairs* 30 (2011), http://op.bna.com/hl.nsf/id/nwel-8dqu2l/$File/Sommerstudy.pdf.
15. Ibid.
16. Ibid.
17. Blackburn and Roe, Real Clear Politics, "Lessons For Health Care Reform," July 22, 2009, http://www.realclearpolitics.com/articles/2009/07/22/tenncare_lessons_for_modern_health_care_reform_97570.html; Blasé, The Heritage Foundation, "Obama's Proposed Medicaid Expansion: Lessons from TennCare," March 3, 2010, http://www.heritage.org/research/reports/2010/03/obamas-proposed-medicaid-expansion-lessons-from-tenncare.
18. Finkelstein, Baicker, et al., "Medicaid Increases Emergency-Department Use: Evidence from Oregon's Health Insurance Experiment," *Science* 17, no. 343 (6168) (January 2014): 263–68. Published online January 2, 2014. doi:10.1126/science.1246183.
19. Sharon Long, "Physicians May Need More Than Higher Reimbursements to Expand Medicaid Participation: Findings from Washington State," *Health Affairs* no. 9 (2013): 1560–67.
20. Ibid.
21. Sandra Decker, "Two-Thirds of Primary Care Physicians Accepted New Medicaid Patients in 2011–12: A Baseline to Measure Future Acceptance Rates," *Health Affairs* 32 (2013): 71183–87.

22. http://www.mcclatchydc.com/2013/05/13/191105/most-doctors-still-reject-medicaid.html.

23. Stephen Zuckerman, Aimee F. Williams, and Karen E. Stockley, "Trends In Medicaid Physician Fees, 2003–2008," *Health Affairs* 28, no. 3 (May/June 2009): 510–19.

24. Bruce Japsen, "Obamacare's 73% Medicaid Pay Raise for Doctors Is Delayed," *Forbes*, March 15, 2013, http://www.forbes.com/sites/brucejapsen/2013/03/15/obamacares-73-medicaid-pay-raise-for-doctors-is-delayed/.

25. Abby Goodnough, "Medicaid Growth Could Advocate Doctor Shortage," *New York Times*, November 28, 2013, http://www.nytimes.com/2013/11/29/us/lack-of-doctors-may-worsen-as-millions-join-medicaid-rolls.html?_r=0&pagewanted=print.

26. Rebecca Adams, "Washington Health Policy Week in Review Medicaid Pay Increase Still Missing in Action in Most Places," *The Commonwealth Fund*, June 3, 2013, http://www.commonwealthfund.org/Newsletters/Washington-Health-Policy-in-Review/2013/Jun/Jun-3-2013/Medicaid-Pay-Increase-Still-Missing-in-Action-in-Most-Places.aspx.

27. Ibid.

28. http://www.texmed.org/template.aspx?id=24764.

29. Denise Grady, "Children on Medicaid Shown to Wait Longer for Care," *New York Times*, June 15, 2011, http://www.nytimes.com/2011/06/16/health/policy/16care.html.

30. "Chapter 58 of the Acts of 2006, an Act Providing Access to Affordable, Quality, Accountable Health Care," Mass. Const., ch. 58, April 12, 2006.

31. Avik Roy, "Emergency Room Visits Increase in Massachusetts," *National Review Online*, July 7, 2010, http://www.nationalreview.com/critical-condition/230795/emergency-room-visits-increase-massachusetts/avik-roy.

32. http://www.nytimes.com/2013/11/29/us/lack-of-doctors-may-worsen-as-millions-join-medicaid-rolls.html?_r=0.

33. Avik Roy, "Emergency Rooms Will Get More Crowded," *National Review*, July 13, 2010, http://www.nationalreview.com/agenda/230979/emergency-rooms-will-get-more-crowded/avik-roy.

34. The examples in this paragraph come from D. M. Fox and H. M. Leichter, "Rationing Care in Oregon: The New Accountability," *Health Affairs* 10, no. 2 (1991): 7–27.

35. Timothy Egan, "Oregon Lists Illnesses by Priority to See Who Gets Medicaid Care," *New York Times*, May 3, 1990, http://www.nytimes.com/1990/05/03/us/oregon-lists-illnesses-by-priority-to-see-who-gets-medicaid-care.html.

36. Ibid.

37. Daniel Calkthan catalogues the ethical challenges posed by such rationing. http://content.healthaffairs.org/cgi/reprint/10/2/78.pdf.

38. Letter noting assisted suicide raises questions; http://abcnews.go.com/Health/story?id=5517492&page=1.

39. Glenn Harlan Reynolds, "Medicaid's Awful Results: Column," *USA Today*, November 11, 2013, http://www.usatoday.com/story/opinion/2013/11/11/obamacare-health-care-obama-medicaid-avik-roy-column/3489067/.

40. http://www.nationalreview.com/articles/313120/medicaid-america-s-worst-health-care-program-avik-roy; http://www.encounterbooks.com/books/how-medicaid-fails-the-poor/.

41. Scott Gottlieb, "Medicaid Is Worse Than No Coverage at All," *Wall Street Journal*, March 10, 2011, http://online.wsj.com/news/articles/SB10001424052748704758904576188280858303612.

42. "Obama's Proposed Medicaid Expansion: Lessons from TennCare," Heritage Foundation, http://www.heritage.org/research/reports/2010/03/obamas-proposed-medicaid-expansion-lessons-from-tenncare.

43. J. K. Giacovelli et al., "Insurance Status Predicts Access to Care and Outcomes of Vascular Disease," *Journal of Vascular Surgery* 48, no. 4 (October 2008): 905–11.

44. R. G. Roetzheim et al., "Effects of Health Insurance and Race on Early Detection of Cancer," *Journal of the National Cancer Institute* 91, no. 16 (August 1999): 1409–15.

45. Siran M. Koroukian, Paul M. Bakaki, and Derek Raghavan, "Survival Disparities by Medicaid Status," *Cancer* 118, no. 17 (December 27, 2011), http://onlinelibrary.wiley.com/doi/10.1002/cncr.27380/full.

46. J. Kwok et al., "The Impact of Health Insurance Status on the Survival of Patients with Head and Neck Cancer," *Cancer* 116, no. 2 (January 2010): 476–85.

47. Damien J. LaPar et al., "Primary Payer Status Affects Mortality for Major Surgical Operations," *Ann Surg* 252, no. 3 (September 2010): 544–51; http://www.nationalreview.com/critical-condition/231147/uva-study-surgical-patients-medicaid-are-13-more-likely-die-those-without-.

48. Ibid.

49. Rachel Rapoport Kelz et al., "Morbidity and Mortality Of Colorectal Carcinoma Surgery Differs by Insurance Status," *Cancer* 101, no. 10 (November 2004): 2187–94.

50. J. G. Allen et al., "Insurance Status Is an Independent Predictor of Long-Term Survival after Lung Transplantation in the United States," *Journal of Heart and Lung Transplantation* 30, no. 1 (January 2011): 45–53.

51. Katherine Baicker et al., "The Oregon Experiment—Effects of Medicaid on Clinical Outcomes," *New England Journal of Medicine* 368 (May 2, 2013): 1713–22, http://www.nejm.org/doi/full/10.1056/NEJMsa1212321.

52. Robert Graboyes, "Medicaid Expansion: States under Duress," *Richmond Times-Dispatch*, November 17, 2013, http://mercatus.org/expert_commentary/medicaid-expansion-states-under-duress.

53. See "Medicaid Expansion: A Morality Issue?," https://www.medicare.com/medicaid/medicaid-expansion-a-morality-issue.html.

54. http://capsules.kaiserhealthnews.org/index.php/2013/11/about-91000-enroll-in-medicaid-as-result-of-aca-woodwork-effect/; http://watchdog.org/65676/mt-bullock-seeks-medicaid-expansion-but-woodwork-effect-could-hurt-state-budget/.

55. http://mercatus.org/publication/american-healthaw-care-system-principles-successful-reform.

56. Healthy Americans Act, http://en.wikipedia.org/wiki/Healthy_Americans_Act.

57. Op cit.

58. Sara Rosenbaum and Benjamin D. Sommers, "Using Medicaid to Buy Private Health Insurance—The Great New Experiment?," *New England Journal of Medicine* 369 (July 4, 2013): 7–9, http://www.nejm.org/doi/full/10.1056/NEJMp1304170.

59. R. Pear, "States Urged to Expand Medicaid with Private Insurance," *New York Times*, March 22, 2013: A14.
60. Robert Graboyes, "American Medicine: Closing of the Frontier?," *USA Today*, November 7, 2013, http://mercatus.org/expert_commentary/american-medicine-closing-frontier.
61. Robert Graboyes, "Paging Dr. Jobs," *McClatchy Tribune*, October 2, 2013, http://mercatus.org/expert_commentary/paging-dr-jobs.

APPENDIX: A MEDICAID TIMELINE

1798	The Marine Hospital Act (1798) became the federal government's first foray into the public provision of health care. Originally designed to benefit seamen, its scope grew, and it became the Public Health Service.
1935	Franklin D. Roosevelt signs Social Security Act.
1964	Lyndon Johnson outlines plans for his War on Poverty legislation during his first State of the Union address.
1965	A Democratic Congress creates Medicare parts A and B and Medicaid programs under Johnson's leadership.
1971	States are permitted to expand Medicaid coverage to elderly or disabled patients in intermediate care facilities and the option to expand coverage to those with mental retardation.
1972	The Social Security Amendments of 1972 create supplemental security income, or cash assistance, for the elderly or disabled. Under these amendments, states must expand Medicaid to cover SSI recipients or expand coverage to those in intermediate care facilities.
1974	Medicaid enrollment reaches 20 million people.
1985–90	Medicaid expands, increasing mandatory eligibility requirements and expanding state coverage options.

1993 States begin expanding Medicaid under section 1115 waivers.

1997 Balanced Budget Act implemented, creating the Children's Health Insurance Program, increasing welfare spending, and cutting Medicare payments to health-care providers.

1998 Medicaid spending increases about 20 percent between 1996 and 1998 in spite of steady enrollment numbers.

2010 Including federal transfer payments, Medicaid accounts for 22 percent of state spending.

2010 Federally subsidized health benefits expand through Affordable Care Act (ACA) and the law encourages states to expand Medicaid to all US citizens and legal residents with income up to 138 percent of the poverty line by covering all of the initial costs of expansion.

2014 Health insurance marketplaces go live; other features of the ACA begin, including expansion of Medicaid and prohibiting insurance coverage due to preexisting health conditions.

ACRONYMS AND ABBREVIATIONS

ACA	Patient Protection and Affordable Care Act
AEI	American Enterprise Institute
AFDC	Aid to Families with Dependent Children
ARRA	American Recovery and Reinvestment Act
CBO	Congressional Budget Office
CHIP	Children's Health Insurance Program
CMS	Centers for Medicare and Medicaid Services
DSH	disproportionate share hospital
FMAP	federal medical assistance percentage
FPL	federal poverty level
FY	fiscal year
GAO	US Government Accountability Office
GDP	gross domestic product
HCFA	Health Care Financing Administration
HHS	Department of Health and Human Services
HIFA	Health Insurance Flexibility and Accountability
HSA	health savings account
IGTs	intergovernmental transfers
NASBO	National Association of State Budget Officers
NHE	national health expenditures
OBRA	Omnibus Budget Reconciliation Agreement
OECD	Organization for Economic Cooperation and Development
OMB	Office of Management and Budget
SSI	Supplemental Security Income
TANF	Temporary Assistance for Needy Families
UPLs	upper payment limits

ABOUT THE CONTRIBUTORS

Joseph Antos is the Wilson H. Taylor Scholar in Health Care and Retirement Policy at the American Enterprise Institute (AEI). He is also a health adviser to the Congressional Budget Office, and he recently completed two terms as a commissioner of the Maryland Health Services Cost Review Commission. Before joining AEI, Antos was assistant director for health and human resources at the Congressional Budget Office and held senior positions in the US Department of Health and Human Services, the Office of Management and Budget, and the President's Council of Economic Advisers.

Charles P. Blahous is a senior research fellow at the Mercatus Center at George Mason University and a public trustee for Social Security and Medicare. He specializes in domestic economic policy and retirement security (with an emphasis on Social Security and employer-provided defined-benefit pensions) as well as in federal fiscal policy, entitlements, demographic change, and healthcare reform. Blahous was named to *SmartMoney*'s "Power 30" list in 2005 and has written for the *Wall Street Journal*, *Washington Post*, *Financial Times*, *Politico*, *National Review*, *Harvard Journal on Legislation*, and *National Affairs*, among others.

Darcy Nikol Bryan, MD, is a practicing obstetrician-gynecologist in Riverside, California. She is a fellow with the American College of Obstetrics and Gynecology, chair of the Maternal Child Department at Riverside Community Hospital, and the former president of the Riverside Medical Clinic Foundation. She is also an assistant clinical professor at the University of California, Riverside. Bryan received her medical degree from the Yale School of Medicine and completed her residency at the UCLA Medical Center.

James C. Capretta is a senior fellow at the Ethics and Public Policy Center and a visiting fellow at the American Enterprise Institute. He studies health-care and entitlement reform, US fiscal policy, and global population aging. From 2001 to 2004, he was an associate director at the White House Office of Management and Budget, where he was responsible for healthcare, Social Security, education, and welfare programs. In addition to his work as a researcher and commentator on public policy, Capretta is a health policy and research consultant.

Jason J. Fichtner is a senior research fellow at the Mercatus Center at George Mason University and an adjunct professor at the Georgetown McCourt School of Public Policy, the Johns Hopkins School of Advanced International Studies, and the Virginia Tech Center for Public Administration and Policy. His research focuses on Social Security, federal tax and budget policy, retirement security, and policy proposals to increase saving and investment. Fichtner served in several positions at the Social Security Administration, including as deputy commissioner of social security (acting), chief economist, and associate commissioner for retirement policy. He also served as senior economist with the Joint Economic Committee of the US Congress.

Robert F. Graboyes is a senior research fellow at the Mercatus Center at George Mason University. He specializes in the economics of health care and holds teaching positions at George Mason University, Virginia Commonwealth University, the George Washington University, and the University of Virginia. Previously, he was a sub-Saharan Africa economist at Chase Manhattan Bank, a regional economist at the Federal Reserve Bank of Richmond, and an economics professor at the University of Richmond. Twice he was a visiting health care scholar in the Republic of Kazakhstan. He has chaired the National Economists Club and the Healthcare Roundtable of the National Association for Business Economics.

Thomas P. Miller is a resident fellow at the American Enterprise Institute. He served as a member of the National Advisory Council for the Agency for Healthcare Research and Quality from 2007 to 2009 and as a senior health policy adviser for the John McCain presidential campaign in 2008. Miller has been a senior health economist for the Joint Economic Committee of the US Congress, director of health policy studies at the Cato Institute, and director of economic policy studies at the Competitive Enterprise Institute. He is the coauthor of *Why ObamaCare Is Wrong for America.*

June O'Neill is the Wollman Professor of Economics at Baruch College, City University of New York (CUNY). She is a research associate of the National Bureau of Economic Research and an adjunct scholar of the American Enterprise Institute. Between 1995 and 1999 she served as director of the Congressional Budget Office. She was elected vice president of the American Economic Association in 1998. Earlier O'Neill held senior-level appointments at the US Commission on Civil Rights, the Urban Institute, the President's Council of Economic Advisers, and the Brookings Institution. Her published articles and books deal with issues related to health, social security, welfare reform, the federal budget, tax policy, and education finance. She was the first chair of the Board of Scientific Counselors of the National Center for Health Statistics. She has also advised state and local governments and private industry on labor and welfare issues.

Nina Owcharenko is the director of the Center for Health Policy Studies. She oversees the Heritage Foundation's research and policy prescriptions on such issues as healthcare reform at the federal and state levels, Medicare and Medicaid, and children's health and prescription drugs. Her research and analysis have been published in newspapers and periodicals around the country, as well as in such noted policy journals as *Health Affairs*. Owcharenko served as legislative director to Sen. Jim DeMint (R-SC) when he was a representative and to Rep. Sue Myrick (R-NC). She began her Hill career on the staff of the late Sen. Jesse Helms (R-NC).

ABOUT THE MERCATUS CENTER AT GEORGE MASON UNIVERSITY

The Mercatus Center at George Mason University is the world's premier university source for market-oriented ideas—bridging the gap between academic ideas and real-world problems.

A university-based research center, Mercatus advances knowledge about how markets work to improve people's lives by training graduate students, conducting research, and applying economics to offer solutions to society's most pressing problems.

Our mission is to generate knowledge and understanding of the institutions that affect the freedom to prosper and to find sustainable solutions that overcome the barriers preventing individuals from living free, prosperous, and peaceful lives.

Founded in 1980, the Mercatus Center is located on George Mason University's Arlington campus.

www.mercatus.org